STRAIGHT WHITE MALE

Norm and Ahmed
Alex Buzo

Radha and Ryan
Nick Parsons

CURRENCY PRESS
The performing arts publisher

CURRENT THEATRE SERIES

First published in 2024
by Currency Press Pty Ltd,
Gadigal Land, Suite 310, 46–56 Kippax Street, Surry Hills, NSW 2010, Australia
enquiries@currency.com.au
www.currency.com.au

in association with The Great South Land Film Company Pty Ltd

Copyright: *Norm and Ahmed* © The Estate of Alex Buzo, 1973, 2024. *Radha and Ryan* © Nick Parsons, 2024.

COPYING FOR EDUCATIONAL PURPOSES

The Australian *Copyright Act 1968* [Act] allows a maximum of one chapter or 10% of this book, whichever is the greater, to be copied by any educational institution for its educational purposes provided that that educational institution [or the body that administers it] has given a remuneration notice to Copyright Agency [CA] under the Act. For details of the CA licence for educational institutions contact CA, 12/66 Goulburn Street, Sydney, NSW, 2000; tel: within Australia 1800 066 844 toll free; outside Australia 61 2 9394 7600; fax: 61 2 9394 7601; email: memberservices@copyright.com.au

COPYING FOR OTHER PURPOSES

Except as permitted under the Act, for example a fair dealing for the purposes of study, research, criticism or review, no part of this book may be reproduced, stored in a retrieval system, or transmitted in any form or by any means without prior written permission. All enquiries should be made to the publisher at the address above. Any performance or public reading of *Straight White Male* is forbidden unless a licence has been received from the authors or the authors' agents. The purchase of this book in no way gives the purchaser the right to perform the plays in public, whether by means of a staged production or a reading. All applications for public performance should be addressed to the authors c/—Currency Press.

Typeset by Brighton Gray for Currency Press.
Cover image by Danielle Evans.

Currency Press acknowledges the Traditional Owners of the Country on which we live and work. We pay our respects to all Aboriginal and Torres Strait Islander Elders, past and present.

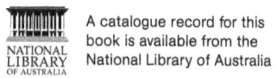
A catalogue record for this book is available from the National Library of Australia

Contents

NORM AND AHMED   1

RADHA AND RYAN   23

Theatre Program at the end of the playtext

Norm and Ahmed
Alex Buzo

Norm and Ahmed was first performed by the Old Tote Theatre Company at the Old Tote Theatre, Sydney, on 9 April 1968, with the following cast:

NORM	Ron Graham
AHMED	Edwin Hodgeman

Director, Jim Sharman
Set Designer, Allan Lees

CHARACTERS

NORM, a strongly-built, middle-aged man.
AHMED, a slim, young Pakistani student.

SETTING

A footpath on a Sydney street under some scaffolding in front of a construction site. A white fence at the back, about five feet high, and then a wire-mesh fence rising above it. The scaffolding is supported by two posts at the front, which are joined by a handrail. There is a bus stop on one side and a garbage bin on the other.

TIME

Midnight on a summer night.

Lights up on NORM, *who is leaning against the fence. He wears an open-necked white shirt and grey trousers. A clock strikes twelve.* NORM *moves around restlessly looking up and down the street. He takes out a cigarette packet, looks in it, then screws it up and flings it on the ground angrily. He brings out a fresh packet, rips off the cellophane with his teeth and takes out a cigarette, which he lights with a lighter. He moves around a bit more and then leans on the fence again. He waits. Then he starts moving around some more, and suddenly straightens up, looking to his left. He puts his cigarette out and takes another from the packet, putting it in his mouth unlit. He leans casually against the fence. The sound of footsteps is heard and* AHMED *appears, wearing a Nehru-style suit and carrying a briefcase. He walks past* NORM.

NORM: Excuse me, mate.

    AHMED *stops and looks at* NORM. *Pause.*

Got a light?

AHMED: Yes, certainly.

    He offers a box of matches.

NORM: Thanks.

    He keeps the matches after he has lit up.

I was dying for a smoke. Lucky you turned up. Nothing open at this hour.

AHMED: No, it's nearly midnight.

    Pause. AHMED *has been waiting for* NORM *to return his matches, but now he starts to edge away warily.*

NORM: Wait a minute, mate.

AHMED: Yes?

    Pause.

NORM: You forgot your matches.

    He holds them out.

AHMED: [*taking them warily*] Thank you.

He edges away.

NORM: What's the matter, mate? Do you think I'm going to hold you up and rob you or something?

AHMED: [*hastily*] Oh no, not at all.

NORM: This isn't India, mate. You're in Sydney. No Bombay stranglers around here. You're quite safe.

AHMED: There are hoodlums here, too. Just as many as in my country.

NORM: Yeah, I'd reckon it'd be about evens. What part of the … uh … south-east Asian sub-continent would you be from?

AHMED: I am from Pakistan. Karachi, to be exact. I, uh, really must be going …

NORM: Eh, wait a minute, mate. I'm not going to rob you or bash you or anything.

AHMED: I was not suggesting for one minute that you were.

NORM: Then what's the matter, you think I'm a drunk? You think I'm one of those old pisspots who go around the place annoying decent people?

AHMED: No, not at all.

NORM: You think I'm a poofter, then, don't you? That's what you're thinking, isn't it? You think I'm like those poofters in Hyde Park who go around soliciting blokes.

AHMED: Certainly not. I assure you I think nothing of the kind. I hope I have not insulted you in any way. If I have, I crave your forgiveness.

NORM: Ar, she's right. I suppose you've got to be careful these days. Lot of nasty types around.

AHMED: Yes, there is a lot of violence prevalent at the moment.

NORM: Too right. You look a bit uneasy.

AHMED: I do?

NORM: Yes. Are you sure you're all right?

AHMED: Yes.

NORM: You don't look all right.

AHMED: I feel fine.

NORM: My name's Norm Gallagher, what's yours?

AHMED: My name is Ahmed. [*Moving away*] Well, I don't wish to seem rude …

NORM: Pleased to meet you, Ahmed.

He offers his hand.

AHMED: [*shaking hands*] How do you do?

NORM: Pakistan. Now that's an interesting place. I've never been to Pakistan. I was in Egypt during the war, but we never went anywhere else. How do you like Australia?

AHMED: It is a very nice place. Naturally I tend to get a little homesick at times, but I quite like it out here. The people are very friendly.

NORM: It's good to hear that, Ahmed. You feel you're settling down all right?

AHMED: Yes, I think so. One always experiences difficulties when one is seeking to adjust to an alien environment. But once the initial period of adjustment is over, it is easier to acclimatise oneself.

Pause.

NORM: That's very true.

AHMED: Yes. Now if you'll excuse me, I'll ...

NORM: Do you know what? You're insulting me, do you know that? Eh? You're insinuating that I'm some kind of drunken pervert.

AHMED: Oh no, you have misconstrued my actions. I think nothing of the kind.

NORM: Then why do you keep backing away, eh? Answer me that.

AHMED: Well ... I mean ... it's late. It's late at night.

NORM: I know it's late. That's no reason. You think you're a bit above me. You don't want to talk to me. I'm insulted. If you think I'm a drunken perv, why don't you say so? Why don't you come right out and say it?

AHMED: I'm very sorry if you think that. Perhaps I have shown bad manners. I offer my humble apologies.

NORM: Never been so insulted in all—

AHMED: Please! Believe me. I did not mean to be rude.

NORM: You sure?

AHMED: Of course I'm sure.

NORM: Well, all right then, don't worry about it. Just a bit of a misunderstanding, that's all. No hard feelings. Jees, I tell you what, Ahmed, you really looked scared there for a minute.

He laughs.

AHMED: [*smiling, relieved*] Did I really?
NORM: [*jovially*] Yeah, you were terrified. You looked as if a kick in the crutch and a cold frankfurt'd finish you off. You're all right now?
AHMED: Yes.
NORM: You sure?
AHMED: Yes.
NORM: No worries?
AHMED: No.
NORM: You sure?
AHMED: Yes.
NORM: Everything's fine?
AHMED: Yes.
Pause.

NORM: You sure?
AHMED: Yes! Yes! I am sure!
NORM: [*prowling around* AHMED] Good. I'm pleased to hear that. That's very encouraging. Where do you live, Ahmed?
AHMED: I am at La Perouse, not far from the university. I'm sharing a flat with some Indian students.
NORM: La Perouse, eh? What, right out at Botany Bay?
AHMED: Yes. The flat overlooks the bay.
NORM: That's where it all started, isn't it? That's where old Captain Cook landed, Botany Bay. Must have given the boongs a fright, eh? I mean, the Aborigines were probably quite surprised to see the white men in their big ships. All those sails in the wind. They probably thought the white man was some kind of monster.
AHMED: That's quite possible.
NORM: You know much about Australian history?
AHMED: No, not a great deal. I am studying it at the university.
NORM: You're out at the old brain-drainer, eh? What course would you be taking, Ahmed?
AHMED: Arts. I am studying for a Bachelor of Arts degree.
NORM: Arts, eh? What, bit of a painter, are you?
AHMED: No, I am not doing painting, I am studying the humanities.

NORM: Oh. Uh ... now just what exactly would that involve, Ahmed?
AHMED: History, mainly. I am majoring in History.
NORM: Oh, History. Yeah, I see. I was never much good at History. No head for dates. That was my trouble. Tell me, Ahmed, what with your education and all, you'd be able to form a few impressions, like, of this country. I mean, you'd be able to sort a few things out. Have your own opinions.
AHMED: Yes, I have formed several opinions of your country ... some good, others bad.
NORM: What would you say was a bad point, Ahmed?
AHMED: Well, I would rather talk about the good points. It would hardly be diplomatic on my part to seek to undermine—
NORM: Ar come on, Ahmed, don't give us that. Don't be a creamer all your life. Tell me a bad point. The White Australia Policy, the way we govern ourselves, anything you like. I want you to tell me, right here and now, what you feel, in your own mind, is a bad thing in this country.
AHMED: Well then, if you are so keen to hear my opinion, I would say that ... uh ... Well, for one thing, one of the, uh, less desirable aspects of your society, to my mind, would be the tendency of the mass media to be merely the mouthpiece of the big commercial and military interests ... the, uh, free press, as it were. They brainwash the people. They ... Oh, please forgive me, I forget myself. As I said, it is not perhaps my place to seek to condemn your country. I have my own opinion, but I do not go around broadcasting it as it would not be the diplomatic thing to do.
NORM: Well, that's fair enough, Ahmed. I can see your point of view. For instance, if I went over to Pakistan, I wouldn't tell you blokes how to run your country. I'd keep it to meself. I wouldn't throw me weight around in someone else's country. Mind you, I'd have me own opinion, though.
AHMED: Ah, that is quite right. I think you have put it most appositely, Norm. I have my own views but I observe a diplomatic silence.
NORM: That's a very sensible idea. I understand exactly how you must feel, Ahmed. When I was in Egypt during the war, I didn't think the Egyptians ran their country extra well. But I kept quiet, I didn't

want to crool meself. And just between you and me and the garbage can, I didn't cotton much to the Egyptians themselves. We had our differences, I can tell you. I never took to them.

AHMED: A difficult race to understand, perhaps. I can readily appreciate the frustrations you must have experienced.

NORM: It's nice of you to say that, Ahmed, because these blokes were hard to understand. There were faults on both sides, of course, and there's two sides to every question, as you well know, but, well, there it is. I just didn't take to them. Might have been my fault. You see, they're a cunning lot, those Gyppos. Take you down as soon as look at you. Some of our blokes were easy pickings for those bastards. Fruit on the sideboard. That's what they were.

AHMED: How long were you over there?

NORM: Quite a while. During the desert campaign. I was in Tobruk, mate. I was one of the Rats of Tobruk.

AHMED: That was quite a battle, wasn't it?

NORM: Yes, it was a pretty good scrap—but we held out, mate, we stuck to our guns. We fought with everything we had—I even knocked one of 'em down with me bare hands. It's true. He was a prisoner, trying to escape, but I apprehended him and jobbed him one. I can still remember that night—I was out for a stroll on the gravel, savouring my last cigarette, when I heard this click in the moonlight, see. So I hid in the shadows and had a screw at the compound. [*Miming*] Then I saw him. It was a Kraut, cutting through the wires, trying to escape from us, the AIF. So I jumped out and confronted him … I offered to take him quietly, but the bastard come at me with a knife. I just stood there, cool as the proverbial cucumber. Then we started circling each other in the dark, round and round and round. [*Circling* AHMED] Then all of a sudden I grabbed him …

He grabs AHMED *by the throat.*

… and I—

He suddenly releases the struggling AHMED, *who breaks away and retreats a few paces, watching* NORM *warily.*

Jees, what have I done? Sorry, Ahmed, old mate. I got a bit carried away there for a minute. Are you all right?

AHMED: [*straightening his collar*] Uh ... yes, I'm all right.
NORM: I just got too excited, Ahmed, and that's a fact. I hope you'll forgive me.
AHMED: [*not quite won over*] Oh, certainly.
NORM: You know how it is, you do your block, you don't know where you are. Sure you're all right?
AHMED: Quite sure.
NORM: What a thing to do! And you a visitor to this country. I don't know what you must think.
AHMED: Oh, don't worry about it, Norm. You got a little excited, that's all.
NORM: You'll probably go back to your country and tell 'em we're all a mob of savages out here.
AHMED: [*profusely*] Not at all, Norm, not at all. I will do nothing of the kind.
NORM: You'll go back there and spread the word that we're all barbarians out here.
AHMED: No, no, I will do no such thing.
NORM: Don't know what came over me.
AHMED: Believe me, Norm, it's all right. No harm has been done.
NORM: You'll forgive me, then?
AHMED: Of course, of course.

> NORM *looks at him, smiles and pats him on the back.*

NORM: Good on you, Ahmed, old mate. You're a good sport. Here, have a cigarette.

> *He offers a packet.*

AHMED: Thank you.

> AHMED *takes a cigarette and puts it in his mouth. He fumbles in his pocket for matches.* NORM *brings out his cigarette lighter and flicks it on.* AHMED *leans over to light his cigarette, but stops a few inches short of the lighter. He looks at the burning flame and then takes the cigarette out of his mouth and looks at* NORM, *who is beaming benignly at him. He looks at the flame again, hesitates, then finally puts the cigarette in his mouth and lights it from the flame.*

NORM: Anyway, Ahmed, as I was telling you, I floored this bloody Kraut. Really laid him out. He was all over the place like a mad woman's lunchbox. just lying there waiting for me to kill him. But do you know what I did?

AHMED: No, Norm, I have no idea.

NORM: I spared him. That's what I did. I could never kill a man in cold blood, Ahmed. It's not in my code of ethics. Not what I call doing the right thing. Human life is sacred, Ahmed, that's my firm belief. So I took him back to the compound and handed him over to the proper authorities without laying a hand on him. I was the hero of the whole battalion after that little effort, I can tell you. I was the toast of Tobruk, and that's the gospel truth. You do believe me, don't you?

AHMED: Why, of course, Norm.

NORM: It's as true as I'm standing here. And if I tell a lie, then may the Good Lord strike me down from above with a bolt from the blue.

He darts an anxious glance upwards.

AHMED: That's very interesting, Norm. But don't you feel that despite your heroic act, the barbarity of war left a scar on you?

NORM: Not a scratch. Of course, I was lucky, luckier than my old man. He was in the Gallipoli campaign, one of the original Anzacs.

Pause.

He fell at Lone Pine.

Pause.

It was a dawn raid. He was killed by a stray bullet. They buried him the same morning.

AHMED: I'm very sorry to hear that.

NORM: Well, that's the way it goes. After all, the price of liberty is eternal vigilance.

AHMED: The price of what?

NORM: Liberty.

AHMED: Oh.

Pause.

NORM: You're not having a go at me, are you?

AHMED: No, not at all. I feel sorry for the Anzacs, poor fellows. However, the Anzac legend is often invoked in support of ... other campaigns. But, forgive me, I am once again posing as a critic of your country. I must again remember that I am a visitor to this land. A thousand apologies.
NORM: That's all right, Ahmed. You've got your views and I respect them. Long as you do the right thing by yourself and other blokes and don't go throwing your weight around, you'll be all right out here.
AHMED: Thank you, Norm, that is very good advice.
NORM: Don't mention it, Ahmed. I like to see blokes like you getting on well out here. All you Asian students coming out here to study and then going back to your own countries, it's a good thing, I reckon. Should be more of it. Mind you, though, not everyone goes along with it. A bloke at work said he didn't see the point of bringing a whole lot of boongs out here. Excuse the term, Ahmed, I'm just giving you a verbatim report, like, of what the bloke at work said. But I had occasion to take him to task when I heard him say that, Ahmed. I said, 'We're forging the bonds of friendship with our Asian neighbours. Knowledge is the key to the door of understanding and friendship', that's what I told him.
AHMED: That's very interesting Norm. But what specific course does this understanding and friendship take?
NORM: Well, you know ... understanding ... and ... being friendly.
AHMED: I see.
NORM: [*quickly*] Anyway, Ahmed, what do you do in your spare time? Got any hobbies, play any sport?
AHMED: No, I don't really have time for that sort of thing.
NORM: No time for sport? Jees, that's a sad state of affairs. I always used to find time to play sport when I was a young feller. I used to play football before the war. Rugby League. I played lock. That was my position, lock. Talk about cover defence! I used to hit 'em hard and low, round the knees, down they went. They can't run without legs, can they? That was my philosophy. But I was always a clean player, Ahmed, I never put the boot in. Always played hard and clean, I was a good sportsman, too. Never sold the dump to

a mate. I always played fair, but if they ever mucked me about, biff! Send for the cleaners. All over bar the shouting. Know what I mean? I remember one bloke. A real coot. Played prop for Balmain Juniors. Tall bloke, he was. A long, thin streak of pelican shit. He tried to hang one on me at Leichhardt Oval once, so I administered a knuckle sandwich to him. He woke up in Our Lady of Mercy Hospital. Should have known better; I always observed the true spirit of the game. Ever played Rugby League, Ahmed?

AHMED: No, unfortunately. I have to spend most of my time studying.

NORM: That's a pity. It's not healthy, you know, to keep your nose stuck in a book all the time.

AHMED: Oh, I don't spend all my time studying. I am compelled to work at night to put myself through university.

NORM: Yeah? Why doesn't your old man send you a few bob to help you along? You wouldn't have to flog your chops too much then.

AHMED: My father is unable to supply me with financial assistance because he, unlike some other people, is not very affluent.

NORM: Jees, that's a bit rough. You've got my sympathy, Ahmed. You must have a pretty tough job, having to work and study at the same time.

AHMED: It is not easy.

NORM: What are you going to do when you finish?

AHMED: When I obtain my degree I intend to return to Pakistan and attempt to render assistance to the under-privileged peoples, perhaps also to undermine the position of the over-privileged peoples. I have some old school friends over there who are dedicated to the cause. I remember when I graduated from secondary school in Pakistan we had a speech day at the end of the year. It was an official ceremony, too, with all the, er, dignitaries, as you say out here. All the top civil servants and military men and businessmen were there on the official dais with the school authorities. As the highlight of the occasion it was arranged that a flock of doves would be released by the big window and would fly out over the playing fields of the school as some sort of symbolic gesture. But unfortunately they took fright at all the lights and the applause and suffered severe indigestion. They flew round and round and round above the dignitaries, bestowing excrement on the Establishment. We all laughed and laughed and some of the boys threw paper darts at the dignitaries. When one boy introduced a fire hose into the proceedings, the situation grew somewhat out of hand. I shall always cherish the memory I have of one bespattered military gentleman crawling around under a table trying to find one of his medals, as the gentle rain from heaven fell all around him. We boys had a great time. It was a mad, wild, exhilarating day, I shall always remember it.

NORM *has been sitting on the handrail during this speech. Now he stands.*

NORM: Yeah, it sounds like a real rort. But, if you don't mind my saying so, Ahmed, in a spirit of friendly criticism, with no malice of forethought, or any offence intended on my part, don't you think your behaviour was a bit on the rough side? I mean, you know, I'd be the last bloke to start defending the bloody dignitaries, and I don't go much on pomp and circumstance and all that sort of garbage, but still, all in all, and looking at both sides of the question, I'd be a bit inclined to say that the blokes who get into these official positions, well, they're pretty important blokes, and I'd say they deserve a little bit of respect from the general public. I mean, I'd be the last one to start putting them up on a pedestal, and if they ever bung on side with me, mate, they know what they can expect. I don't take no crap from no-one. But, by the same token, and taking all things into consideration, I reckon that if a bloke's in an official capacity, like those blokes who came to your school, well, it's only fair that he should earn a little bit of respect.

AHMED: I fear I must disagree with you there, Norm. I do not regard these accursed officials with perhaps the same reverence as you do. We shall overthrow them! We demand social justice! Oh, I beg your pardon, Norm, I fear I was carried away there for a moment. I hope you will excuse my excessive zeal.

NORM: Ar, she's right, Ahmed. But just remember what I said. Anyway, I hope you get through uni all right, so you can go back to your country and do whatever it is you want to do. As a matter of fact, I've got a son at uni. Young Bernie. He's studying in America. He's at the MIT—the Massachusetts Institute of Technology.

AHMED: What's he studying?

NORM: Well … technology, you know? He's got an assured future in front of him, my Bernie, he'll be a leader in science and industry—he's got the qualifications, you see. He's a real cluey bloke, no risk. We were very proud of him when he graduated from Sydney Uni. It was an official ceremony. All the dignitaries were there … the Governor, the Premier and the Governor-General, all up there on the official dais with all the other authorities. What a magnificent sight! Bernie wasn't nervous. He came through fine. It was a very impressive ceremony.

AHMED: It must have been a proud moment for you, Norm.

NORM: Yes, it certainly was. Bernie's the only one in our family with a university degree. None of the rest of us are all that bright. But the Gallaghers are getting on, mate. My old man was a factory worker, I'm a white-collar worker, and now Bernie's a technologist. Things are looking up, I tell you.

AHMED: What kind of white-collar work do you do, Norm?

NORM: Well, er, actually I'm a storeman, like, in a warehouse. But I wear a white shirt and tie under me dustcoat, though. I mean, I'm not sort of technically a white-collar worker, but I wear a white collar, y'see? I mean, there's a bit of a fine distinction involved in this. Y'see, I'm not always in the warehouse—I spend a lot of time in the office, checking invoices and rectifying a few anomalies.

AHMED: Ah, I see. It sounds very complicated.

NORM: Yes, it's a funny business. But I'm doing all right for meself. Making a bit of money, got a nice big house, everything laid on, I'm doing fine. But there's just one thing wrong, Ahmed.

AHMED: What's that?

NORM: Well, you see, Ahmed, I'm all alone now, since my good wife Beryl passed away to the heavens above.

AHMED: I'm very sorry to hear that, Norm, you must be rather lonely.

NORM: That I am, Ahmed, that I am. Sometimes when I'm out in the backyard, watering the frangipanis, I feel very lonely, I really do. Now that dear Beryl's in another world I don't know where I am. She was a lovely woman, a real beauty in her day, jet-black hair, sparkling eyes, and an ear for music. Played a good game of bowls in her twilight years. But now she's gone and where am I? Up the creek without a paddle! It's the good times I miss, Ahmed, those magic moments that make life seem worthwhile. Like the time we danced all night at the Bronte RSL. Yes, I really miss dear old Beryl, with her happy laugh, her way with kids, her curried eggs on toast of a winter's night. But now, Ahmed, now I sit at home alone and think of yesteryear.

AHMED: That is most unfortunate, Norm. But surely you must have some human contact, some form of social intercourse?

NORM: Oh yeah, my daughter Lorraine comes round and cooks me roast dinner of a Sunday. But she's married, you see, she's got her own life to lead. She made a good catch, that girl. Got on to a real go-ahead type. Young Gary. He's in the retail business, you know. Runs a hot dog stand at Harold Park. Got his eye on a kiosk at Miranda. No flies on Gary, mate, you mark my words. Fine-looking young feller, too. Very tall, with big broad shoulders and a good head for figures. Likes a dash of lemon in his Resch's. He comes around and takes me out to the football sometimes. I get a little lonely, you see, being all alone. I like to get out and do something, meet some people. I like to have a nice chat with a bloke, find out how he's getting on in the world. A bloke like you, for instance, Ahmed. A visitor to our shores. A young citizen from the south-east Asian sub-continent.

AHMED: Well … I hope I can … I mean … if I can be of … any … that is, I …

NORM: Step over here a minute, will you?

Pause.

AHMED: What?

They look at each other.

NORM: Just step over here for a minute.

Pause.

AHMED: Why?

NORM: What's the matter, Ahmed? Come here.

AHMED *moves warily closer to* NORM.

Over here. Under the light.

AHMED *moves closer.*

AHMED: What do you want?

NORM *surveys* AHMED.

NORM: Just as I thought.

Pause.

You haven't really got such a dark skin, have you?

AHMED: A dark skin? What do you mean?

NORM: I mean you're not a black, are you? You could pass for a Greek or a Turk. You've got more of an olive complexion.

AHMED: What are you getting at? I fail to understand …

NORM *laughs. He moves out from the shadows.*

NORM: Don't get upset, Ahmed. Don't do your block. I was only thinking that if you didn't have a dark skin you'd be all right. I mean, it'd be all right for you to stay here, like, get a job and stay in this country. But you haven't really got a dark skin, have you? It's sort of olive coloured. They'd never call you 'Mr Midnight', would they?

AHMED: Some would.

NORM: Eh, come on Ahmed, now don't have a wetty. No offence meant. You're not angry, are you? Eh?

AHMED: No, it's all right, Norm, I'm not offended.

NORM: Good. We're still mates, then. I suppose you'd have a right to get touchy about that sort of thing. I wouldn't blame you for getting touchy. I can see your point of view.

AHMED: Thank you, Norm. I appreciate your concern.

NORM: She's right, Ahmed. I tell you what, in this world we've got to learn to understand the problems of others and not worry too much about our own.

AHMED: That is very true, Norm. You seem to possess a most humanitarian outlook on life.

NORM: I'm very flattered, Ahmed, to hear you say that. In this world there's too many blokes getting in for their chop and not worrying about their mates. You'd appreciate that, I mean, being a historian and all.

AHMED: Uh, yes, I suppose I would.
NORM: You know, as I was saying, Ahmed, you could do all right for yourself if you stayed out here. After you got your degree, you could stay here and be a useful asset. I mean, as I said, you're not really black, so you wouldn't have that much trouble.
AHMED: Well, perhaps. I shall have to obtain my degree before I consider a proposal of that nature.
NORM: That's fair enough. First things first, after all. But give it a bit of thought, Ahmed. You'd be welcome out here, I can vouch for that. The people'd treat you just like one of their own, no risk. You'd be all right. No worries there. You could make your way in the world out here.
AHMED: Yes, it is a most attractive proposition.
NORM: You could have a good time out here, Ahmed. It's an easy life. Take this morning, for instance. On Sunday mornings I sit out on the terrace and sip a Tia Maria and read the sports section. Lorraine's in the kitchen, smell of a roast lamb on the breeze, what more could you want? Green lawns all around, vista of the harbour, Holden in the garage, I'm sweet. No worries. See what I'm getting at? You wouldn't have that in Pakistan, now would you? You could set yourself up very nicely out here. There's lots to recommend it, believe you me. It's a bloody good set-up, take my tip. Look at me. I've got a good job, good pay—I'm doing all right. A reliable firm, nice personnel. You know who I had a beer with on Friday?
AHMED: No, Norm, I have no idea. Who?
NORM: I had a beer with the man himself, the Managing Director, my boss. [*Filled with awe*] I drank with the Managing Director of the firm.
AHMED: That must have been … an experience.
NORM: He shouted a round, too, just like any ordinary bloke would. He took a shine to me, too, I could see that. He was very impressed with me. It was a most cordial affair. I know how to conduct meself on these occasions. Not like my old man. Do you know what he had?
AHMED: What?
NORM: He had a criminal record. It's true. My mother told me. He was put away for a while.

AHMED: What did he do?

NORM: He bashed up his boss. Yes, that's right, bashed up his boss. It's ... inconceivable, that's what it is. Talk about a blot on the family record. It's a stain on the Gallagher escutcheon. The memory of it still haunts me. It's enough to make you want to chuck, isn't it? 'Course, you wouldn't find that sort of thing around these days. Rare as a pregnant nun. That's progress for you. We've cut that sort of thing out.

AHMED: Yes, it would indeed be a rare occurrence in contemporary times.

NORM: Too right. Yes, he was a real ratbag, my old man. Mad Dan Gallagher, they used to call him. Always getting into fights and organising strikes and things. He died just before I was born. My mother nearly had a miscarriage when she heard the news, but she got over it all right. I arrived safe and sound. She used to tell me about him when I was a young feller. He was always holding meetings in our living room. Then they'd all go into the kitchen and my mother would make them a cup of tea. All big men they were, with horny hands and sturdy braces. My mother was real tiny. They'd pick her up and whirl her round and round and round the room and when they were drunk they'd sing 'I'll Take You Home Again, Kathleen' or 'The Wild Colonial Boy'. There was a whole mob of them—Flanigan, Hanigan, Branigan, Lanigan, O'Toole, O'Riley and Schultz. Then one night the cops raided the place and took them away. They were all singing 'Sweet Adeline' in the black maria. What a bunch of ratbags they were! Some of them used to come round after the war to see my mother. I was only a kid then. They gave me some liquorice. We lost touch with them after a while. It was a bit before my time, all that. I got dim memories ... like ... long time ago ... bit cloudy ... Wobbly bastards!

> NORM *kicks over the garbage can in a fit of anger.* AHMED *is a bit startled, but doesn't move.*

Jees, there I go again, doing me block. Excuse me, Ahmed, but my old man does make me angry. He had no respect for law and order and common decency.

AHMED: Perhaps it is sometimes desirable to effect an alteration in the status quo.

NORM: Could be. But my old man wanted to change things, Ahmed, he tried to buck the system. You can't do that.

AHMED: Not in this country, at any rate.

NORM: No fear. Anyway, they got onto him pretty quick. The policemen came around and took him away, but not before he'd bashed one of them up. An officer of the law. Disgraceful! It's like I told you, he had no respect for law and order, and that's a terrible thing.

AHMED: Oh, I don't know, sometimes I feel the police deserve some form of retaliation from their victims.

NORM: Ar, come on, Ahmed, give the copper a fair go. They're not such bad blokes. Give them a break. They're just doing their job, that's all. They only want to preserve law and order in the community. Mind you, though, if a mug copper ever started pushing me around, I'd job him good and proper, no risk about that. I don't take no crap from no-one. But, by the same token, Ahmed, I reckon our policemen are doing a pretty good job and I'd do all that's in my power, all that's humanly possible, to assist them in the performance of their duties. Go easy on the old wallopers, that's what I say, give the coppers a fair go.

AHMED: Well, I think they get a pretty fair go. I observed one beating up an old drunk earlier this evening. For no reason, either. It was sheer brutality.

NORM: Now come on, Ahmed, the policemen do a good job keeping all the drunks and pervs off the streets and making them safe for decent citizens. These blokes are a menace, you know, especially the pervs. Ever been solicited, Ahmed?

AHMED: No, I have not been accorded that distinction.

NORM: Well, you want to watch out for that sort of thing. It could happen any time.

AHMED: Yes, I'm certain it could.

NORM: Yes, any time, any time at all. Pervs aren't choosy, you know. Some of these blokes'll drop their tweeds for a ripe banana. I saw an old perv in Centennial Park last week. He was having a tug in the gutter, going at it hammer and tongs. He must have been hard up, eh?

AHMED: Uh … yes.

NORM: You ever get like that, Ahmed? Eh? Do you?

AHMED: No.

NORM: Never get hard up?

AHMED: No.

NORM: Never had a tug in the gutter?

AHMED: Certainly not. I hardly think a public thoroughfare is a suitable venue for conducting autonomous experiments of that nature.

Pause.

NORM: You got a funny way of putting things, Ahmed.

AHMED: You find my syntax humorous?

NORM: No, not humorous, Ahmed. Just funny. I suppose you get a lot of people who admit you speak better than they do, eh? I bet a lot of people say you speak better than the average native-born Australian.

AHMED: Yes, I have been paid that compliment.

NORM: Yes, I could very well … envisage that. But anyway, Ahmed, that's just another reason why you should settle down out here—there's no language barrier. You could live here very … autonomously. You're not like all those chows down in Dixon Street that jabber away in Chinese half the time. You can speak the Queen's English. You know, you could really make something of yourself if you stayed out here, Ahmed. Look at my boss, for instance.

AHMED: That Managing Director fellow?

NORM: Yes. He was telling me about the struggles he's had to establish his great enterprise. It wasn't easy, he said, in the early days. It was hard at first, but he won through in the end. It was a stirring struggle, but one man's dream came true. He became a legend in his own lifetime. He challenged the gods and carved out a name for himself that will survive in the annals of human endeavour. But that's the sort of thing that happens in this country, Ahmed. You could have a success story like that, you know. Start off with a billycart and finish up with a fleet of Boeing 727s.

AHMED: Perhaps. I have not given much thought to—

NORM: You could settle down, get a house in a nice suburb with lots of trees and birds and things. A place where you can wash the car of a Saturday and do a bit of gardening of a Sunday. Do you like gardening, Ahmed?

AHMED: It is indeed a pleasant pastime. I like to—

NORM: That's for sure. There's nothing I like better than to get out in the garden of a Sunday. Put me amongst the hydrangeas and I'm at peace with the world. When there's a breeze in the palms and the sun's getting low, I get out in the yard and get stuck into the weeds. I weed away to my heart's content. I couldn't ask for any more in this world or the next, and that's my solemn oath. It's the simple pleasures, Ahmed, that make this life worth living. Sometimes when I'm on my way home from church of a Sunday night, when the strains of the last hymn have died and the humble pilgrims have gone home to bed, I stop and look up at the stars in the sky and think what a wonderful world it is we live in. But, by the same token, Ahmed, I do miss the old days a bit. The times when we used to sit around the fire with our friends and sing all night. There was real warmth between people in those days. We were like brothers, all getting stuck into the grog together. And when I was out in the bush and I stopped at a pub, I knew every bloke in the place within five minutes. Community feeling, that's what it was; community feeling. We used to have it in the old days. And when I sit home of a night, all by myself, I open a can of DA and think back over my life. The happy, happy times, like when the young fellers started calling on Lorraine. She was a lovely girl. Dead spit of Beryl, she was. She—ar jees, Ahmed, look, I'm sorry to carry on like this. I don't know what you must think.

AHMED: Oh, no, Norm, you go right ahead.

NORM: Sorry to crap on so much, Ahmed. I don't know what came over me. It's just that I don't get much of a chance to talk to people these days. And I do like a bit of a yarn, I really do. Just to talk to someone, that's all I want. And when I do find someone to talk to, I just mag away like an old woman and ruin everything.

AHMED: You say whatever you want to, Norm, I don't mind.

NORM: I just crap on and spoil it all.

AHMED: No you don't, Norm. I have been listening, believe me.

NORM: You mean that, Ahmed?

AHMED: Of course I mean it.

NORM: Good on you, Ahmed, you're a real human being. I don't suppose it's easy to put up with an old bludger like me.

AHMED: On the contrary, Norm, it has been most interesting to meet you.

NORM: Thanks, old mate, that's very nice of you, to say that. Well, I'd better let you go now, Ahmed. But just before you go, I would like to say this from the very bottom of my heart, that I wish you every success in the world. And I do hope you get on well out here. Now you're sure you're settling down all right?

AHMED: Oh yes, I'm making my way.

NORM: I'm glad to hear it, Ahmed. I wouldn't like to think of you as being lonely. You see, I'm on my own, too, and I know what it's like. A young bloke your age ought to be out and about, mixing with people, getting amongst the girls. You know what your trouble is, Ahmed, don't you?

AHMED: What?

NORM: You're too shy. That's the first thing I noticed about you. You're too shy.

AHMED: You think so?

NORM: Of course. It's obvious.

AHMED: It is true that I do not have many friends.

NORM: Look, I tell you what, Ahmed. Why don't you go up to the New South Wales Leagues Club and have a good time? Mention my name to the bloke on the door and you'll be in like the proverbial Flynn. Just tell 'em Norm sent you, that's all you have to do. Go up with your mates and get on the hops. You'll soon get to know the blokes up there. A great mob they are, too. I've got a feeling they'll take to you, Ahmed, I think you'll go down well.

AHMED: Thank you, Norm, I shall bear that in mind.

NORM: You do that, Ahmed, you do that. I'd like to see you meeting some people, making some friends. Loneliness is a terrible curse, Ahmed, and I'd like to see you coming out of your shell. We're not such a bad mob out here, you know. We might be a bit on the rough-and-ready side, but our heart's in the right place.

AHMED: Oh, I have had ample proof of that.

NORM: And as I said, Ahmed, you really ought to give a thought to staying out here. Find yourself a good woman, something more than just a weekend root, and settle down and raise a family. Buy a weekender on the coast, join the local leagues club—ever been to a leagues club, Ahmed?

AHMED: No, I have that pleasure in front of me.

NORM: Fabulous places. They've improved a lot, these clubs. Twenty years ago they weren't much chop, just a place to go when you wanted to get out on the grog. But now, jees, what a difference! They go in for amenities a lot these days, for the comfort of the patrons. They're very well-appointed, these clubs, very well-appointed. Anyway, Ahmed, there it is. Good prospects, you could have a good time, what more could you ask for? This place'd be made for a bloke like you.

AHMED: Well, I think I will concentrate on completing my tertiary education first. My primary concern is to obtain a liberal education and my secondary concern is to gain a deeper understanding of human behaviour.

NORM: Ah ... yes, that's fair enough. But keep it in mind, Ahmed, we'd love to have you. And the people—they'd take you to their hearts. Everyone from Alice Springs to breakfast time. It'll be a red carpet job.

AHMED: Thank you very much, Norm, that is very nice of you. I must say I have received some warm hospitality from a lot of people since I have been in your country. It has been most gratifying. Of course, uh, not everyone has extended this hospitality towards visitors from eastern backgrounds, such as myself.

NORM: Ar well, you've got to take the rough with the smooth. There's ratbags wherever you go. But the majority of people'll do the right thing. I think you'll go down well out here.

AHMED: Thank you again, Norm. I certainly hope so. You have given me something to think about.

NORM: Glad to hear it. Well, Ahmed, I must say it's been a pleasure to meet you and have this little talk. I mean, to reach a common understanding. That's what the world needs, I reckon, a bit of common understanding.

AHMED: That is very true. I have enjoyed meeting you, too, Norm, it has been a real pleasure.

NORM: Put 'er there, mate.

He offers his hand.

AHMED: [*reaching out to shake hands*] Yes, I—

NORM punches AHMED in the stomach, then in the face. He grabs AHMED's head and bashes it against the post. Then he flings the limp body over the handrail.

NORM: Fuckin' boong.

The clock strikes one.

Blackout.

THE END

Radha and Ryan
Nick Parsons

Acknowledgements

I would like to express my heartfelt thanks to the late Kevin Jackson for his early guidance, to my daughter Adelash Parsons for help with being young and female, to Michael Briggs for his insights into crisis counselling, and, for advice on trans matters, to Darby Carr and Sebastian Kaye. Thanks in particular to Darby for his incisive brain and apparently endless patience, tolerance and kindness.

Radha and Ryan was first performed at La Mama HQ, Melbourne, on 24 April 2024, with the following cast:

RADHA	Gursimar Kaur
RYAN	Sam Eade
BOYD	Danny McGinlay

Director, Nick Parsons
Designer, Joanna Arrowsmith
Lighting Designer, Max Bowyer
Sound Designer, Mikaela Innes
Music, Thomas Smith

CHARACTERS

RADHA, early twenties.
RYAN, mid-thirties.
BOYD, mid-twenties.

SETTING

An inner-city bus stop, around 2.00 a.m.

This play text went to press before the end of rehearsals and may differ from the play as performed.

A bus stop, early hours of Sunday morning. The bus shelter is lost in shadow. Music from a dance party is drifting in.

RADHA *totters on, moderately drunk, moderately high. She's dressed as an anime character, Saki Watanabe—a kind of cute sailor suit—and her skin is sprinkled with sparkles.*

She peers at the bus timetable, pulls her phone from a tiny shoulder bag and checks the time.

RADHA: Fuck.

> *She calls from her 'Favourites' menu. As she rings, the glow of a cigarette appears in the shadow of the bus shelter. The call goes to voicemail.*

Mags … pick up your fucking phone! … I need a lift!

> *She hangs up in disgust.*

Bitch.

> *She looks at her phone again. Maybe she should call an Uber …*

RYAN: You need a ride?

> RADHA *yelps.* RYAN *emerges from the shadows.*

Shit. Sorry … I thought you saw me.

RADHA: What are you doing here?

RYAN: [*gesturing with his cigarette*] Waiting for my Uber. There's no buses.

RADHA: I know.

RYAN: You wanna share?

> *She looks at him.*

RADHA: No …

RYAN: No, seriously, you'll be waiting all night. Where are you headed?

RADHA: Surry Hills.

> *She immediately regrets it.*

RYAN: Sweet. It's on the way. I'll pay; it's fine.

RADHA: It's not that.

> *Pause.*

RYAN: Hey, I am the last person you need to worry about. Honestly. I was just sitting here, you turn up ... you look like you need a ride. That's it.

She takes another look at him. Starts to relax a little.

RADHA: Okay.
RYAN: I'm Ryan. We met at the party.
RADHA: Did we?
RYAN: Well ... we collided. I remember your um ... How come you're dressed like that?
RADHA: Oh ... I'm Saki Watanabe. Meant to be.
RYAN: Saki Watanabe?
RADHA: Yeah ... *From the New World*.
RYAN: Right ... What new world?
RADHA: It's anime. A series. *From the New World*. About this kind of utopia where everyone has psychic powers.
RYAN: Okay. Right ... So ... you always dress like her? Or ... ?
RADHA: I came from another party. It had a theme.
RYAN: Right. Anime.
RADHA: Cosplay. So ... yeah.
RYAN: Cool.

Beat.

And you are ... ?
RADHA: Sorry! I'm Radha.
RYAN: Nice to meet you. [*Offering the cigarette pack*] Smoke ... ?
RADHA: No. Thanks.
RYAN: [*putting the pack away*] Smart. So ...

He tries to gauge the moment.

Look ... thing is ... I had a bit of a ... bust-up with my girlfriend.
RADHA: Your girlfriend?
RYAN: Yeah.

Silence.

You thought I was gay.
RADHA: I'm so sorry.
RYAN: Why? ... Don't worry. Everybody thinks that. But I'm ... I really need to call her. I said some ... I need to make amends.

RADHA*'s defences are instantly back up.*

I would really like to borrow your phone. If that's okay. Just for a minute.
RADHA: Where's your phone?
RYAN: Died.
RADHA: You called an Uber.

He takes a breath.

RYAN: I called an Uber. Then it died.

She holds on to her phone.

One minute.
RADHA: Why don't you call her tomorrow?
RYAN: Aaah … You know what they say: never let the sun go down on an argument.

She looks at him warily. It's taking all his self-control not to just grab the phone.

Please.

Beat.

I'm trying to save my relationship.

Pause.

All right, fine. Sorry.

He sits in the bus shelter.

RADHA: What's her name?
RYAN: Her name?
RADHA: Your girlfriend.
RYAN: You don't believe I have a girlfriend.
RADHA: I don't know you.
RYAN: What the fuck is wrong … with our world?

Beat.

Her name is Pia.

She looks at him uncertainly.

RADHA: It's two a.m. You should talk to her tomorrow.
RYAN: No! Tomorrow it'll all be messed up again. I need to … say it now. While everything is … I've got a list of like … five things that I need her to know, tonight, when it's clear. When it's in my head.
RADHA: Still not a good idea.

RYAN: [*snapping*] I do not need your fucking advice!

She freezes and he takes the phone from her hand. He swipes up and holds it in front of her face to unlock it, then makes a call. RADHA *stares.*

I'm sorry. I'm so sorry; I don't act like …

The phone answers—but goes to voicemail.

I … Fuck! … [*After the beep*] Hey, it's me.

Long pause. He can't think of anything to say.

Call me back, all right?

He hangs up, stares hopelessly at the phone.

RADHA: I really can't see why you've got problems.

He looks at her.

Give me back my phone.

RYAN: She's calling me back.

RADHA: What?

RYAN: She might call back.

RADHA: What the fuck is wrong with you? Give me the fucking phone.

He looks at her, torn.

She's not calling you back, fuckhead. Just give—

The phone starts buzzing in his hand. He stares at the screen. Beat.

RYAN: It's your mum.

RADHA *snatches the phone, sends the call to voicemail and starts to walk off.*

Hey! … You just hung up on your mum!

RADHA: Fuck off!

He runs around, cuts her off.

RYAN: Hey, I'm sorry … I'm sorry—fuck—please, I really didn't mean to freak you out.

RADHA: Well, you fucking did.

RYAN: I know, but I'm … I need you to know that I'm not … I'm not like this.

She moves past him.

Come on, I'm sorry, where you going?
RADHA: Home!
RYAN: Well, that's miles away. Isn't your girlfriend coming to pick you up? What'd you call her? 'Mags'?
RADHA: Yeah ... I don't know.
RYAN: Hold up, hold up ... you're half-cut, it's dark as fuck and Surry Hills would be an hour's walk at least. Come on. Let me drop you off. Just to say thanks and ... and I'm sorry. [*Moving away*] I'll stand all the way over here. We can use sign language.

She looks at him uncertainly.

Or ... go back to the party. I'll come and get you when it arrives. Seriously. Very least I can do.

She glances back at the party.

RADHA: No ... I'll wait here.
RYAN: So ... that's a yes?

Beat.

RADHA: Sure. Thanks.
RYAN: Okay.

Beat. RYAN *looks at her, looks back at the party.*

Something wrong?
RADHA: I'm just tired.
RYAN: [*trying to lighten the mood, making air quotes*] 'Tired and emotional'?
RADHA: What?
RYAN: Euphemism.
RADHA: I feel a bit sick.

An awkward pause.

RYAN: I'm really sorry about the phone.
RADHA: Forget it.

Silence. RYAN *tries to fill it.*

RYAN: So ... 'Radha'. Where's that from?
RADHA: What d'you mean?

RYAN: Aaah … I dunno, just, what's your background?
RADHA: Why do people always ask that?
RYAN: I don't know! I'm just … It's a pretty name.

She looks at her phone, looks at him.

RADHA: My dad's Indian. It means 'success'.
RYAN: Right. Nice.
RADHA: And she's a …
RYAN: 'She's a …'?
RADHA: Nothing. It just—It means 'success'.
RYAN: 'She's a' … What? She's a goddess.
RADHA: Yeah.
RYAN: An Indian goddess. Of … ? Come on. You have to tell me now.

She looks at him, annoyed.

RADHA: Love.
RYAN: Love. Nice.

Pause.

RADHA: No comment?
RYAN: Nope.
RADHA: Nothing suggestive?
RYAN: It's a nice name.

Silence.

RADHA: What happened with your girlfriend?
RYAN: Ah. Rule one-oh-one.
RADHA: What's rule one-oh-one?
RYAN: 'When changing the subject, make it about him and he will never notice.' You seem expert at that one.

She looks away, stifling a smile.

RADHA: Now you're changing the subject.
RYAN: Oooh. Well spotted.

He looks, trying to assess her.

Pia's … at the end of the road, that's all.
RADHA: Short road, was it?
RYAN: Aaah, six … and-a-half years.

RADHA is a little taken aback, regrets her flippancy.

She doesn't find me attractive.

RADHA: Wow. Candid.

RYAN: Yeah.

RADHA: Where is she now?

RYAN: [*nodding*] At the party.

RADHA: Oh.

RYAN: All I did was put my arm around her. Doesn't like me 'pawing' her is how she put it.

RADHA: That's harsh.

He shrugs, puffs on the last of his cigarette, stubs it out.

RYAN: Yeah … I dunno. They say once the sex is gone, it's over.

RADHA: Sex isn't everything. Once the whole … horny 'being in love' part fades, you have to build on something else.

RYAN: Ah. Romantic. Such as?

RADHA: Trust and communication. Men suck at those.

RYAN: I get it. This is my fault.

RADHA: Mmm, I didn't say that, but … you did just get defensive.

He looks at her. What?

Poor communication.

RYAN *snorts.*

I'm just saying … most men are locked down emotionally. Maybe it's something to look at.

RYAN: Right. Noted. Thanks for that.

RADHA: You're welcome.

RYAN: Why do women always think men can't talk about their emotions?

RADHA: I don't know. Bitter experience?

RYAN: What you mean is, we don't talk about *your* emotions.

RADHA: I don't mean that at all.

RYAN: We must have dated different people. Even now if I tell Pia how I feel, it always—it somehow turns into a conversation about how *she* feels. You know, I'm like, 'Pia, I'm having a panic attack' and she's like, 'Oh, my God, that makes me so depressed'.

RADHA: Sounds to me like Pia's a narcissist.

RYAN: That's your diagnosis.

    RADHA *shrugs*.

RADHA: I don't know her.

RYAN: She's just normal. Pop-feminism aside, talking as a guy, what women want is someone stoic who has their shit together, doesn't need emotional support, but is always emotionally available to them.

RADHA: What? Come on. That's a generalisation. Some men are sensitive, some women won't be.

RYAN: Right. So there's an overlap.

RADHA: Of course.

RYAN: So I might not be an emotional cripple.

    She laughs.

RADHA: Shut up! I didn't … I would never say that!

RYAN: Seriously. I managed a bar for a while and my rule number one: if you want to get laid, never talk about yourself. Talk about *her*.

RADHA: [*wryly*] Is that how it works?

    He shrugs.

RYAN: Not saying it's bad. Just how it works. You say men have a tendency not to talk about their feelings, I say women have a tendency not to want to hear about it. And to be honest, I wouldn't want to hear about my feelings either. So why don't we say that both things are true?

RADHA: [*smiling*] You are such a boy.

RYAN: Working on it.

    Pause.

You should call your mum back.

    RADHA *shakes her head, scowls.*

What?

RADHA: I'll call her later.

RYAN: Your mum doesn't call you at two in the morning unless she's worried.

RADHA: Well, she can worry.

RYAN: Ouch.

    Beat.

You don't live at home, then.
RADHA: [*annoyed*] No, I live with my friends.
RYAN: Okay, fine! ... You have a crazy mum.

Pause.

RADHA: Is it really over? With your girlfriend?

He takes a deep breath. Shrugs.

Maybe ... you know, tomorrow—
RYAN: It is time ... I stopped kidding myself.

She looks at him.

Haven't said that out loud.
RADHA: I'm sorry.

He shrugs, turns away.

RYAN: I think she kind of mistook me for someone else. And I ... can't be that person.
RADHA: You have to be yourself.
RYAN: You hit that on the head.

Beat.

[*Changing the subject*] So ... you come with anyone?
RADHA: Oh, fuck, here we go.
RYAN: What'd I say now?
RADHA: You mean, do I have a boyfriend?
RYAN: I'm just ... asking.

She looks at him.

Do you?
RADHA: If someone says they're feeling sick, they're probably not looking to hook up.
RYAN: I didn't ... think you were, I just—I thought I saw you with someone.

She looks at him. Yeah, right.

RADHA: A friend of Magan's. I met him at the other party.
RYAN: With the theme.
RADHA: Yeah, but it was a bit dead and he was going on to this one ...
RYAN: Right.

RADHA: He seemed really nice.
RYAN: Ah. But … ?
RADHA: Nothing. I'm …
RYAN: Gotcha. You're tired.

Pause.

So what's going on with your mum? Seriously.
RADHA: [*scrabbling in her purse*] I don't want to talk about it.
RYAN: Oi. Trust and communication, right?

She grimaces at him.

RADHA: How close is that Uber?
RYAN: Dunno. My phone's dead.

She comes up with a joint, can't find her lighter.

RADHA: You got a light?
RYAN: Ah, yeah …

He produces a silver lighter, hesitates.

You gunna be okay?
RADHA: Just light it.

He does. She draws back, offers him a toke. He hesitates, but the truth is he needs it as much as she does. He takes a drag, hands it back. She looks up and down the street.

RYAN: Listen, you're probably safer out here than I am, so … you know, relax.
RADHA: I doubt that.
RYAN: No, that's true! Men are twice as likely to be assaulted.
RADHA: Where'd you get that from?
RYAN: The ABS. Bureau of Statistics. Look it up.

She's sceptical.

You're more at risk in your own home, believe me. You live with someone?
RADHA: I share a house.
RYAN: You said. With a man?
RADHA: With … three other people. A girl and a couple. A straight couple.
RYAN: Ah. Straight, eh?

RADHA: I mean … yes, there is a man.
RYAN: Right. But … not your partner.
RADHA: [*wryly amused*] No.
RYAN: Cool.

>*Beat.*

You a student?
RADHA: Why? Do I look like one?
RYAN: You do, actually.
RADHA: Communications. UTS.
RYAN: Well, there you go. There's a thesis topic.
RADHA: What?
RYAN: 'The lies told to women.'

>*She stares at him. Seriously?*

'Why do women live in fear, and who benefits? Discuss.'

>*She snorts.*

What?
RADHA: Well, I don't think we are being lied to.
RYAN: No? Showing a lot of faith in the patriarchy.

>*She looks at him.*

No, fair enough.
RADHA: Violence against women is a real thing.
RYAN: Yeah. It is. Sorry. [*Indicating the joint*] Don't give me any more of that.

>*Beat.*

RADHA: All right, just tell me. Who benefits?
RYAN: Look … I'm a guy at a bus stop in the middle of the night. You're a little stoned, worried about your safety. I don't want to argue about whether you have a right to feel afraid.
RADHA: Okay. Thank you.
RYAN: You're welcome.
RADHA: For not trying to mansplain me out of my feelings.
RYAN: Absolutely.
RADHA: But … just, what the fuck are you talking about?

>RYAN *shuffles uncomfortably.*

RYAN: This is the shit that gets me in trouble with my friends.
RADHA: [*describing an imaginary bubble around them*] Safe space. Even for me, so you say. So go.
RYAN: Okay, so … All those one-punch assaults that were in the news a few years back: how many victims were female?

RADHA has to think.

RADHA: I don't know. None?
RYAN: Exactly. Men are twice as likely to get assaulted in a public place than women. But men, or—or straight men anyway … walk around at night like they own the joint. And women do not. So what's going on?
RADHA: Men … aren't afraid of sexual assault.
RYAN: That's true.
RADHA: The stakes are higher. It's a worse crime.
RYAN: But where do sexual assaults happen? In private. And almost always it's someone you know. You afraid to go home? No.

He gestures at the empty street.

RADHA: So you're saying you never get nervous. Alone at night.
RYAN: Oh, *I* do, like you said, I look gay, and that's a whole other story. But you know, guys who pass for straight.

She looks at him.

RADHA: Well … men just assume they can defend themselves. It's different.
RYAN: So we're just a bit delusional.
RADHA: Men look for conflict. Women don't.
RYAN: Mmm. Depends on what you mean by conflict.
RADHA: Oh, come on.
RYAN: You never been bullied by a woman?

She gives him an ironic look.

RADHA: I mean physical conflict.
RYAN: Okay. But … like … even so, historically, we do live in a very safe society. If you're male or female.
RADHA: It doesn't feel that safe.
RYAN: That's my point. So, who benefits?

She looks at him.

See? Now I'm in trouble.

RADHA: It's just a weird thing to say.

RYAN: Oh, people believe weirder shit than that. Who really brought down the Twin Towers? ... Is climate change a hoax? Who is Q? ... Conspiracy theories are all bullshit but in every case there is someone who benefits. Someone in plain sight, like oil companies, Vladimir Putin ...

RADHA: How could anyone benefit from making women feel unsafe?

RYAN: Oh! Who would want to control women? I dunno. Let's start a list. How about our entire social framework?

RADHA: Ah, no, too general. Specifically.

RYAN: Specifically? How about every media outlet ever? Female victim, nice big photo ... plenty of clicks. Male victim ... not so much. So they promote the stories that get the clicks, and suddenly it looks to the world like women are the only victims of violent crime.

RADHA: Okay, you are starting to freak me out a little bit.

RYAN: And I said I didn't wanna have this conversation. I'm just saying ... you might be safer than you think you are.

RADHA: [*making air quotes*] In our safe space.

RYAN: Super-safe!

> *Beat.*

RADHA: If more men were really being killed than women, the media would be going crazy.

RYAN: But we are. And they're not.

RADHA: Says you.

RYAN: Google it.

> *She looks at him.*

RADHA: Oh, my God, I've just realised!

RYAN: What?

RADHA: You are Q!

RYAN: Shit. You're deep state, aren't you?

> *They find this funnier than it should be. The joint is kicking in.*

> [*Speaking into his collar*] Donald ... Donald, they got me, you're on your own ...

RADHA: You know what I think?

RYAN: Surprise me.

RADHA: The media likes to cover stories about female victims because the media is run by men.

RYAN: Oooh ... Nice. But ... doesn't really follow.

RADHA: Why not?

RYAN: Because like I said, conspiracies are bullshit; it's always about money. It doesn't matter what gender Rupert Murdoch is. Stories about female victims rate higher because we're hard-wired to care about women more than men. It's in our DNA.

RADHA: What? That—That is bullshit!

RYAN: It's ... It's evolution. You don't need a lot of men to propagate the species so we can afford to lose a few. Fuck, even I don't really care that much about men, if I'm honest. If I hear a woman was killed in a park at night it hits me in the gut. If I hear a man was killed I just think ... 'He was probably in a gang.' It's just the way we are.

RADHA: But ... hang on, you just said that society wants to control women.

RYAN: It does. Because women are more valuable.

RADHA: That is absolutely bullshit.

RYAN: Really? ... I don't see any midnight vigils for men killed on their way home at night. And yet it happens more often to men than to women.

RADHA: If we cared about women more than men ... then women would have the power in society.

RYAN: No, that's not ... what I'm saying. Men do have more, um ... social capital. But they're expendable.

RADHA: That is ... doesn't make sense.

RYAN: Well ... men have most of the dirty jobs, men do most of the dangerous jobs, men do most of the fighting in wars, men have the worst health outcomes, they have a shorter lifespan ... What am I missing?

RADHA: How about that most of our parliament is men, almost all our CEOs and top public servants are men ... men have the highest incomes, the most property, they get more superannuation? ... What am *I* missing?

RYAN: Men have status, but not value. That's all I'm saying. Fuck, they even kill *themselves* at three times the rate of women.

RADHA: Men kill *everyone* more than women do ... Men are violent fucks. No offence. And let's not forget the rapes. And domestic violence.

RYAN: I'm not saying men are not perpetrators. They are. Overwhelming.

RADHA: Then ... what are we arguing about?

RYAN: I'm saying ... 'male violence against women' is—is really just male violence. Men assault other men more than they assault women—that includes gay men, trans men ... They kill each other more than they kill women. And they kill themselves more than they kill anybody else.

RADHA: But ... hang on. That's not right.

RYAN: How d'you mean?

RADHA: Because domestic violence is different ... Before a man kills a woman, he's been bashing her for years. Like, we know that.

RYAN: Yeah, true.

RADHA: So your numbers on assault ... are bullshit. You get mugged in the street, that's one instance. One report. A woman living with abuse, she's been assaulted dozens of times before it gets to the cops. And if there's sexual violence involved then the effect is just magnified out of control.

RYAN: Yeah, maybe ...

RADHA: Not maybe. Fact.

RYAN: But most men don't report assaults either. Especially sexual assault. So. We don't really know.

She looks at him.

RADHA: Well, maybe that means the world is not as safe as you say it is.

RYAN: Aaah ... okay, but there is no epidemic of misogyny out there. There is a problem with frustrated, angry men getting violent.

RADHA: [*sitting on the kerb*] Yeah, well ... there's a distinction without a difference. Who the fuck cares?

RYAN: Right there: ... that is the problem.

RADHA: What have men got to be angry about?

He shrugs, joins her on the kerb.

Seriously. You have everything your own way. You're born male in this country, everything arrives on a fucking silver golf cart.

RYAN: You mean if you're born straight, white and male.
RADHA: Straight white male, yeah. Well, you're a straight white male.
RYAN: Sure.
RADHA: So what are you angry about?
RYAN: It's a mystery.
RADHA: *I* have a right to be angry.
RYAN: Yeah.

They share a tug on the joint.

I'll give you one more stat and then I'll shut up. Ninety-two percent of the prison population is male. Does that seem right to you?

RADHA *looks at him.*

I mean, sixty-five, seventy percent, maybe … But ninety-two?
RADHA: They do ninety-two percent of the crime.
RYAN: Okay … So if you're Indigenous you are eight times more likely to be in jail than non-Indigenous. So they're committing eight times as much crime as everybody else?
RADHA: Don't fucking … That is *completely* …
RYAN: So there is institutional bias in one case but no institutional bias in the other.
RADHA: You are not going to convince me that straight white men have a bias against themselves.
RYAN: It's not straight white men, it's everybody! … Male incarceration rates are not even on the radar. Can you think of any other demographic where we wouldn't be asking ourselves, you know, 'What's going wrong? Is it our education system? Is it rehabilitation?' There are people *inside* the system who ask those questions but … you know, in the marketplace of ideas, all I hear is that it's time we got tough on crime. Again. Which really means, 'Let's lock up *more* men … Even more. Because men are the problem.'

She stares at him.

RADHA: I think you're trying to fucking gaslight me. Mr Q-Anon.
RYAN: Dunno. Is that different to cognitive dissonance?
RADHA: You're saying … men have all the social capital … but the system is biased against men.
RYAN: Sounds a little crazy when you say it like that.

RADHA: You're doing my head in.

She takes a drag, hands him the joint.

Where do you get this shit, anyway?

RYAN: It's an interest. [*Handing back the joint*] I don't normally say it out loud.

RADHA: I'll bet.

RYAN: I guess I'm kinda wondering ... and this is gunna sound really binary, but it's been on my mind ...

RADHA: Fucking just say it.

RYAN: Safe space?

RADHA: So fucking safe.

RYAN: What if these roles that men and women play ... what if it's like ... partly evolution? Like ... we have different bodies. On average. Men are bigger in the upper body—

RADHA: Says you! What do you weigh?

RYAN: I dunno.

RADHA: Sixty kilos?

RYAN: Whatever. I'm just saying ... I dunno what I'm saying. I do know what I'm saying. Why wouldn't our brains be different too? Men have evolved over millions of years to be kind of ... service drones for the family. Men are violent because once upon a time violence had a purpose. It was how men ... brought home food, protected the family and ... But now there's no kind of purpose to it. Men are redundant.

RADHA: That does sound really binary.

RYAN: Yeah, I know. But that's not ... We can *be* anything we want. DNA is not destiny. History is not destiny. But maybe if we—

RADHA's phone buzzes. She checks the caller, groans ... considers rejecting it but ... She turns away from RYAN.

RADHA: Mum! Will you just go to bed? ... Well, don't! I'm fine! ... Yes, I'm at a party; it's—it's a normal party ... I'm getting my own drinks, okay? No-one is buying me drinks ... A friend is driving me ... I don't know. I don't want to see you right now ... No! I'm safe; that's all you need to know ...

She listens, staring at the sky.

Mum—Mum, is he there? ... I can hear him in the background. Is he listening?

Her mother gets half-way through her answer when RADHA *hangs up.*

Fuck.

RYAN: You okay?

She shrugs.

So ... you really don't live at home?

RADHA: No! I haven't been home for a month.

RYAN: Right.

Beat.

So ... a month. Who—? Who's the guy in the background?

She looks at him.

Look, who'm I gunna tell? Right? I'm guessing he's the boyfriend.

She hesitates, but it's been eating at her.

RADHA: He's not her boyfriend; he's ... I don't know. My dad only moved out three months ago.

RYAN: Wow. Okay.

RADHA: He's ... her ...

RYAN: Side hustle?

RADHA: Yeah, something like that.

RYAN: How long has that been going on?

RADHA: I don't know ... They met at uni, so ...

RYAN: They met at uni?

RADHA: Yeah.

RYAN: So ... When was that?

RADHA: Nineteen ... nineties, I dunno.

RYAN: So ... like, thirty years?

RADHA: I don't know! ... Maybe.

RYAN: And you didn't know.

RADHA: No! He's just ... Uncle Paul. He's always been around.

Beat.

RYAN: And your dad didn't know?

She starts to tear up. RYAN *moves to comfort her, thinks better of it. She takes a final drag on the joint, tosses it away.*

Okay, yeah … so … that just up-ended reality. Where's your dad now?
RADHA: He's rented a flat. It's horrible.
RYAN: Are they talking?
RADHA: Yeah.
RYAN: Well, that's good, right?
RADHA: He's not angry! I wish he was angry!

    RYAN *looks at her.*

RYAN: Like you.
RADHA: Yes, like me!
RYAN: You don't want your dad to be jealous. I know what jealous men can do and … believe me, what you've got is better.

    She looks at him.

Don't go to your share house. Go see your mum.
RADHA: No! No way! I can't even look at her.
RYAN: Okay.
RADHA: She cheated on my dad for—for … I don't know; my whole life? I don't know what to do with that.
RYAN: Yeah … well … that is … that's complicated.
RADHA: How could she … ? I mean, she's been living a lie all this time.
RYAN: Radha … she maybe lied to you, but for sure your dad knew. He's always known.
RADHA: What? Why—? Why would you say that? You don't know anything about it!
RYAN: Well … I know two things: this has been going on for as long as you've been alive, and now it's come out, your dad's not angry about it. So … the idea that he knew: that's not a stretch. Which means they've all been hiding it from you all this time. Which is the real reason you're angry.

    He tries to gauge her level of emotion.

Look, I—I'm not—I get that this is terrible. What they did to you is terrible. But there is worse shit in the world, right? And whatever else, it's obvious they care about you. My advice: go home and … don't take sides. Just tell them to work it out.

RADHA: You mean the three of them.
RYAN: Well ... yeah.
RADHA: Her solution would be a thrupple. Can't see dad opting for that.

> RYAN *snorts, tries to stifle a giggle. She looks sideways at him.*

It's not funny.
RYAN: You ah ... You sure he hasn't already been there?
RADHA: [*slapping at him*] Ew! Fuck off! That is disgusting.

> *He falls backwards, laughs at the night sky. She looks at him ruefully.*

Where is this Uber?
RYAN: I don't know ... Listen, I am sorry about ... what's happened.

> *They look at each other.*

RADHA: You know what I think?
RYAN: Surprise me.
RADHA: I think you should stop trying to live up to ... your ... idea ... of manhood.
RYAN: Yeah? What idea?
RADHA: You know! The sort of working-class-hero thing you have going on.
RYAN: Ah ...
RADHA: A bit rough on the outside but ... inside, sort of chivalrous. Brave. A bit paternalistic. Dispensing wise words to young women.

> *He smiles uncomfortably.*

You gotta stop it.
RYAN: [*sitting up*] Why's that?
RADHA: Because there is no place in our world for that man anymore.
RYAN: You don't think?
RADHA: No. He's gotta take off his glasses.
RYAN: Oh, right ... And those glasses would be ... ?
RADHA: The glasses of white male privilege.

> *He looks at her.*

RYAN: For fuck sake.
RADHA: Oh, you think that doesn't exist either?
RYAN: What happened to our safe space?

RADHA: Oh, not feeling safe? Welcome to my world.
RYAN: What d'you know about what I think a man is?
RADHA: You've been telling me for half an hour what a man is! How misunderstood you all are. How you evolved to protect the family! You know how offensive that is?

    RYAN *stands.*

It is exactly your idea of manhood that has led to a gender pay gap that will maybe close up in another twenty-six years! That's led to a quarter of women suffering harassment at work and to homelessness growing fastest for women over fifty-five! Thanks to your idea of manhood, as a young woman the only thing that I feel doesn't really exist are my *actual* prospects!
RYAN: Yeah, I think you might be barking up the wrong tree, mate.
RADHA: I know a straight, white male when I see one.
RYAN: And that defines me, does it?
RADHA: It's your privilege that defines you.
RYAN: Oh … fuck, yeah, I'm so privileged.
RADHA: Well, aren't you?
RYAN: Sure! Yeah, I work my arse off in a dead-end job for bugger all; I'm so privileged I don't own a house and I got no way of getting one … Yeah, I'm just kicking back on Easy Street. Gimme a break.
RADHA: It's not about—
RYAN: My dad worked with his hands all his life. Car detailing, panel beating, construction … if you needed anything made, he could make it. He could build you a fucking actual fridge. From scratch. But he still lost our house when Mum got cancer because … you know, cancer is expensive. She died when she was forty-four, but you know what? Dad was so privileged he got to bring us up on his own. And pretty soon I'll be privileged not to inherit anything except … my memories of him. Sure. I'm just wallowing in it.

    She says nothing. He moves around her.

But I guess you … haven't had my advantages, have you? I mean, not white, not male … More brown. Or … olive? How would you describe your skin?

    She's silent.

You're Indian, right?

RADHA: Australian. Actually. My dad's Indian. My mum's Scottish.

RYAN: So, sorry about that; half Indian, half Scottish, all Aussie … No white privilege for you, then. Poor little Indian love goddess.

RADHA: Get fucked.

RYAN: Nice. They say brevity is the soul of wit.

She stands, almost walks. Decides to stand her ground.

RADHA: White privilege … is not about class.

RYAN: Yeah? … Well, that's a relief because we pretty-much scotched that idea.

RADHA: It's about belonging. It's about going for a job or … applying for a passport and knowing you have a right to it because you are in the club. You belong.

He stares at her.

RYAN: How do you know I belong anywhere?

RADHA: It's still different.

RYAN: Is that right?

RADHA: I will always be an outsider. And you won't.

RYAN: You sure about that?

RADHA: Didn't you hear yourself? 'Half Indian, half Scottish' … That's a card you can play any time. And you played it like a pro. Happy?

RYAN: Oh, whereas you made me feel like a bunch of roses. You and your communications degree. But I'm the one with the privilege.

RADHA: White privilege is a real thing. And so is racism.

He looks away. Pause.

RYAN: White privilege does not define me. And race doesn't define you.

RADHA: Says the white guy with the privilege.

Beat.

Point of difference, then.

Pause.

RYAN: Got another joint?

She stares at him for a moment, searches in her bag.

RADHA: Lucky last.

He lights it for her.

RYAN: You been back to India?

RADHA: I didn't go back. I was born here.

He grimaces.

RYAN: Okay, fuck, look, I'm sorry. I'm not in a good space right now.

RADHA: That makes two of us.

RYAN: I'm feeling … pretty shithouse. So, the privilege thing triggered me a bit.

She looks at him.

RADHA: Me too.

RYAN: Safe space?

RADHA: Safe space.

Beat.

RYAN: Pia said I will never be loved.

RADHA: What?

RYAN: Yeah, she just … put it out there.

He shrugs.

RADHA: She is a fucking bitch, man. I'm sorry, that crosses a line.

RYAN: Even if I'm unreconstructed? And male?

RADHA: Fucking who cares? You don't say that to people.

He looks at her, smiles. He likes her.

RYAN: [*with exaggerated casualness*] So, Radha.

RADHA: Yes, Ryan?

RYAN: You been to India?

RADHA: I have, Ryan! I've been to Jaipur. My family's there.

RYAN: Oh, wow. And how was that? Was it like … coming home, or … ?

RADHA: Aaah … No. No, it wasn't. It's weird. Over there I feel like a white person. But then … coming home, I still miss it.

RYAN: How's that?

RADHA: Don't know. I miss the food.

RYAN: Mmm.

RADHA: Actually … I miss the hospitality. The way they welcome a guest, they draw people in … the way food is part of that. Anglo culture is more insular. We don't take care of each other in the same way. So I miss it but the same time ... I was always the guest. Never ... really one of them.

RYAN: So, what? You can't speak Indian?

RADHA: Hindi.

RYAN: Sorry. Hindi.

RADHA: Not really. A few words. My dad sort of tried to teach me, but ... when you're little you just ... you want to fit in.

RYAN: Yeah, I get that.

RADHA: Now I wish I'd let him. I'm an Oreo. Brown on the outside, white on the inside.

RYAN: A coconut.

RADHA: Yeah.

RYAN: I've got an Islander mate; he says that. But not in a good way.

RADHA: Well, that's ... how I feel, yeah. An Oreo but not in a good way.

Pause.

RYAN: So is your dad helping you out? Financially, I mean. While you're at uni.

RADHA: Yeah.

RYAN: Puts a lot of weight on your education.

RADHA: Yep. My dad is the full Indian stereotype.

RYAN: Yeah, see I love my dad but he couldn't see the need for education.

Beat.

RADHA: Did—? Did you want to study?

RYAN: Yeah ... probably, but it—it wasn't on my radar. I mean, my dad left school in Year Ten, so ... what was I gunna do? Tell him the life he made wasn't good enough? That he shoulda made more of himself? ... None of my mates went to uni ... Actually, one did. We thought he was a wanker. But to be honest, even if I said I wanted to Dad could never afford it. We lived out west, so ... no way I could live at home. And I couldn't pay rent *and* study and pay fees, so ...

RADHA: So it wasn't race, then. Or gender. That cut off your options. It was class.

He looks at her.

RYAN: What're you saying? I got no class?

RADHA: No! I'm—I'm talking about …

He snorts. She sees him grinning.

You are such an arsehole.

RYAN: I'm an enigma.

RADHA: Oh … you mean a black void in our knowledge. So, a cosmic arsehole.

RYAN: And yet you want to share my Uber.

She looks at him ruefully.

I'm not actually racist.

RADHA: Said every racist ever.

RYAN: I think we just learned you might be a bit classist. What about that?

She looks at him sideways.

So … when you've got your degree in Communications … what then?

She shrugs.

RADHA: Journalism maybe. Some kind of writing.

RYAN: Nice to have options.

Beat.

RADHA: You really … never studied?

RYAN: How d'you mean?

RADHA: Well, you say things like, 'Brevity is the soul of wit', you know all these stats, but you don't know the language they speak in Jaipur.

RYAN: Maybe I'm an autodidact.

RADHA: [*smiling*] 'Autodidact'.

Stoned giggling. It takes a while to settle.

RYAN: What're you going to write about? Fiction or nonfiction?

RADHA: Maybe I'll write about you.

RYAN: Good choice. The misogynist, racist, underpaid, working-class autodidact.

She coughs on her joint, cackles.

Am I the hero or the villain?

RADHA: I don't know ... I don't know. What do you actually do?
RYAN: What do I *actually* do?
RADHA: Who's underpaying you?

He looks at her a little warily, takes the joint.

RYAN: Ah ... let's skip that one.
RADHA: Really? Why?
RYAN: Just ... I don't know.
RADHA: What?
RYAN: [*handing back the joint*] Fuck ... I haven't ... had a conversation like this for a—a long time.
RADHA: What are you? A spy? Come on! I've told you everything about me.
RYAN: You'll laugh, though.
RADHA: Fuck, no! ... I'd never laugh at someone's profession.
RYAN: You will. It's the context.
RADHA: The context?
RYAN: Yeah.

Beat. She composes herself.

RADHA: Safe space.

He looks at her sceptically.

RYAN: I'm a crisis counsellor.

She cracks up and despite himself he starts giggling as well.

RADHA: With those opinions?
RYAN: My opinions don't come into it! Fuck. It's not just abused women, you know; I could talk to the men who bashed them. People who are suicidal. People on drugs. Diverse backgrounds ... whoever calls, they get support. It's not my job to pass judgement.

She looks at him.

RADHA: Are you serious? You're really a counsellor.

He shrugs.

I ... Okay, I'm impressed. I don't even know how you do a job like that.
RYAN: Me neither. To be honest, every shift I get anxiety, but ... mostly it's just ... people get lonely. If you're laid up on your own with

chronic pain, who do you talk to? ... I had one old guy ring up about his shopping list. I just listen and ... if they need it I refer to the right service. The main thing is to be on their side. You can challenge but never confront.

RADHA: Oh, like you didn't confront me.

RYAN: You're not a client.

She looks at him, puts a hand on his arm.

RADHA: I think that's really ... something.

RYAN: Thanks.

Awkward pause.

RADHA: Have you ever ... had someone ... try to kill themselves?

RYAN: Yeah ... I've had clients take an overdose.

RADHA: What'd you do?

RYAN: You find out what they've taken, you get an address and you get 'em to open the front door. For the ambos, in case they pass out. One time, I had a woman call up in a DV situation and I was doing the whole 'Are you safe?', 'Is he there?' routine and her partner came home while she was talking and I heard him bashing into her.

RADHA: Oh, fuck! ... Oh, God, that would've been awful. What happened? You called the police.

RYAN: Yeah.

RADHA: Was she okay?

RYAN: That ... is a question I do not ask. Because ... what if she wasn't? ... I still gotta come back and do it again tomorrow. So.

Pause.

RADHA: That sounds like a good way to get PTSD.

RYAN: It's happened. Not to me. Yet. But the agency is pretty good. They monitor the calls and ... I did a debrief with my super. Listened to a lot of loud music. Moved on.

Beat.

RADHA: Hang on ... you ... Don't you need a degree or something to be a crisis counsellor?

RYAN: Yeah, I got one in social work.

RADHA: You said you didn't have an education!

RYAN: No, I said it wasn't a priority for my dad. I did a unit a time while I was managing a bar. Took me ten years. Then Covid hit and … hospo was fucked, so … But, boom-times for crisis counsellors, hey?
RADHA: Fuck. Why … social work?
RYAN: It's cheap. And I could do it online. Mostly.
RADHA: That's the only reason?

> *He shrugs.*

RYAN: Couldn't see myself running a bar at forty.

> *Beat.*

Anyway, I wouldn't call it an education. I know a lot about … a few things. Not much about anything else.
RADHA: Not sure about that.

> *She looks at him sympathetically.*

You are not unloveable.

> *They stare at each other.* RADHA *looks at the joint in her fingers.*

One toke left.
RYAN: You have it.
RADHA: We could share.

> *He looks at her. She drags back on the last of the joint, then leans in and he inhales her smoke. He breathes it out, looking at her. She smiles, moves in to kiss him. He moves back.*

What?

> *He looks at her.*

Come on. You've been flirting all night.
RYAN: I just … I know.
RADHA: Is it Pia?
RYAN: No. I mean … kind of.
RADHA: That's cool. You don't have to explain.
RYAN: No, I … I like you. So …
RADHA: So?

> *Beat. She takes out her phone.*

Why don't you give me your number?

RYAN: Before I … start handing out contact details, I just … wanna be sure that you're clear.

Beat.

RADHA: About what? You're married? What?
RYAN: I'm trans.

She stares at him.

I was born female.
RADHA: Oh! … Trans. Right. Wow.
RYAN: You didn't guess.
RADHA: No! … I mean … Sorry, I was about to say, 'Are you sure?' but that would be …
RYAN: It's fine.
RADHA: Really, really dumb.

Beat.

Oh, my God, I can see … I can see it now. You were really pretty.
RYAN: [*looking away*] Mmm.
RADHA: I mean, you are. Still. Handsome. I mean.
RYAN: Sure.
RADHA: I don't know what to say!
RYAN: It's okay! … It just … It's invalidating, that's all. When I was living as a woman I didn't feel pretty. I felt like a man … in drag. You know, pretending. I know … you're being nice but it—it just—
RADHA: I'm so sorry.
RYAN: Don't be. I'm just … sick of explaining.
RADHA: Yeah … Yeah. I get it.

Beat.

Sorry. You're my first trans person.
RYAN: Yeah … if you think about it, that's probably not true either.

Pause.

RADHA: No … Right. Shit. [*Looking around*] Have you seen my hole? I'd like to crawl into it now.
RYAN: Don't. It's …
RADHA: I know. 'It's fine'.
RYAN: It is fine. Really.

Pause.

RADHA: Thank you.

RYAN: What for?

RADHA: I don't know. Not cis-shaming me. Trusting me, I guess. Someone you only met an hour ago.

RYAN: Don't thank me. Ask me for my number.

She hesitates. He looks away.

Yeah. It's okay.

RADHA: No, I … I … Oh, God. I need … time to process.

He looks at her.

RYAN: All right. Go on.

She looks at him.

Ask.

RADHA: Ask?

RYAN: You can't process without information.

He shrugs.

What do you want to know? Anything you like.

RADHA: Anything?

RYAN: Safe space.

Beat.

RADHA: When—? When did you … ?

RYAN: When did I know?

RADHA: Yeah.

RYAN: Well, it wasn't … like, there was not a day that I woke up and thought, 'Wow, hey, I'm a boy!'

RADHA: No. I guess …

RYAN: The thing about being trans is—is … you have to come out twice. You know? Like, once is hard enough.

RADHA: You—You were gay.

RYAN: Yeah, I was a lesbian. Like, gold star. Massive dyke.

RADHA: Oh, shit.

RYAN: I figured that out on the footy field. Like, back home it's a big sporting town, so there was a couple of girls' teams. And I just …

realised that there was more going on when I tackled some chick than … you know, just getting 'em on the ground.

 RADHA *smiles.*

So, yeah, news flash: lotta lesbians in a girls' footy team. So I got that one sorted pretty early. Came out to Dad first. He was actually great about it … Always known, or so he says. Bit harder with some of the family. And school was a … fucking … well, you know: country town.

RADHA: Really?

RYAN: Things might've changed, I dunno. But kids bully each other; they'll pick on anything, so … you say you're a lesbian in high school, there's always gunna be someone who hears, 'Kick me'.

RADHA: Yeah.

RYAN: You get picked on?

RADHA: Um … a little bit. A lot of brown kids at my school, though.

RYAN: Mmm. Brave new world, I guess. So, you know that bar I was managing? Gay bar, obviously. I was heavily into the scene. And first I was like, 'I've found my people'. I was getting laid all the time; it was great. I was making up for all the years at school feeling 'wrong'. Met Pia. And she was great. We were happy. I guess. It— It really took … a few years before … It's hard to explain, but … I still felt 'off'. Somehow. And the idea of … 'Maybe I'm not … really a girl' … sort of coalesced in my brain. And then one day I told Pia, and … then, suddenly, it was real.

RADHA: Wow.

RYAN: Next question?

RADHA: Oh … please don't.

RYAN: What?

RADHA: I'm sorry. You're not some … sort of …

RYAN: Sideshow attraction?

RADHA: No! … Information service. It's not fair. And I would like your number. If—If that's okay.

 He grins, pulls out his phone.

RYAN: Give me yours; I'll text it to you.

RADHA: I thought your phone was dead.

He looks at her. Oh, shit.

RYAN: Yeah ... sorry. I—I ah—

RADHA: Wait ... Wait. What is this?

RYAN: I—I'm sorry. I—I wanted to borrow your phone. It was easier than trying to explain.

RADHA: Explain what?

RYAN: That I was ... Pia's not taking my calls. I thought if it was someone else's phone, she might pick up. It was stupid. I don't normally ... No, that's not true. I do hide things. I'm not that honest ... with people.

He looks at her, puts his phone away.

I'll just type it in, hey.

He holds out his hand. She unlocks her phone and hands it over. He types in his name and number.

RADHA: Is—? Is that ... why you and Pia ... broke up? Because you're trans?

He blows out a long breath.

RYAN: I—I dunno. I dunno what's in her head. I mean ... she was fine, for a long time ... But I guess we were all on the diversity bandwagon, so she's not going to throw up her hands in horror. You know? It was all, 'You fall in love with the person, not the gender' ... 'You have to do what's right for you' ... blah, blah ... But ... Yeah, so it took me years to realise the bleeding fucking obvious. I'd been living as part of this community on the cutting edge of diversity politics ... many of whom feel marginalised for all sorts of reasons ... and here was me, turning myself bit by bit into a straight white bloke. Traitor to the cause, you know? So ... I dunno. Maybe.

He hands back the phone. Beat.

I remember the actual night it hit me. We used to have these ... slam-poetry nights, you know? Open mike. They were great. I used to get up and do these really edgy ... sort of—well, I thought they were edgy; these poems about ... following some chick in the street and looking at her arse and thinking 'Fuck, she is hot', you know ...

And I used to get these whistles and whooping out of the crowd. I mean, like two hundred people going 'Yeah!' It was like I was putting into words what ... It's like we were validating each other, you know? We were all together in this ... sexy kind of sweaty muddle ...

Beat.

Then one night I got up, and I'd started to grow the beard ... and I did the same kind of material ... and ... but ... I just bombed, you know? The atmosphere was different. They just ... And I realised I wasn't edgy and cool anymore. I was sleazy. A sleazy straight guy talking about women's arses. Like they were reading me differently ... and that changed the meaning of everything I said.

RADHA: That's amazing. And ... kind of sad.

RYAN: Yeah, and I hadn't changed myself—I mean who I was ... but they had changed me. That was my first ... real hint of—of what it's actually like to live as a straight man. And I am no ally of cisgender men, right? I'm definitely not on that bus. But before T ... you'd probably say I was a hard-line feminist. Borderline man-hater. Which is ironic.

RADHA: Misandrist.

RYAN: Misandrist?

RADHA: A man hater: misandrist. Misogynist hates women. Misanthrope hates everybody.

RYAN: How come everybody knows 'misogynist' but no-one knows what a misandrist is?

RADHA: Maybe there just aren't enough misandrists out there.

Beat.

RYAN: You could work on that.

RADHA: I don't hate men. I'm ... I'm angry at them. That's all.

RYAN: Even your dad?

Beat.

RADHA: No.

RYAN: Little bit. Angry at him for not being angry.

RADHA: Yeah, that's true.

RYAN: Bit of support there for the patriarchy. Institution of marriage. Women as property and stuff.

RADHA: Oh, fuck off.

    Beat.

How come you're not still angry? You know what it's like to be female. Being trans doesn't make that shit go away.

RYAN: No. I am still angry, but … I guess when I started passing as a man I started seeing more of their point of view. I mean, this is stupid, but instead of just reacting to stuff I started thinking, 'If that comment came from a woman, how would I feel?' … and that one thing made me just … cut 'em a little more slack.

RADHA: But … if you're trans it's even worse, right? Discrimination and assaults on trans people are—are, like …

RYAN: Standing here, I am six times more likely to get assaulted than you are. I think; data's a little sketchy.

RADHA: Yeah, so … what are you even doing out here?

RYAN: I don't have a right to be here?

RADHA: No, of course! But … I mean, I get nervous. If I were you I'd … I'd be …

RYAN: But you're forgetting my masculine disregard for danger.

    She looks at him.

RADHA: I don't get it! I don't get why you're not more angry than I am!

RYAN: I am! I am so fucking angry! I'm angry about … casual abuse and threats and … I'm angry that I don't really feel safe in a public place. I don't want to 'pass' for male, as though just being a boy is a special club that I don't have the right to join. I just want to be!

    Pause.

But then … when you *do* pass, where people just *assume* … that's when you—you start to realise that the social rules really are different for men. The fact I hadn't really thought about it tells me how insidious binary thinking is. Not just for cisgender men but for all of us. So, yes, trans men and women come in for a lot of violence because we are a walking repudiation of the norm. And we shouldn't and I'm angry at that, but … the norm is also … kind of what I want. So figure that one out.

    Pause.

Yeah. So, obviously, I chucked it in at my gay bar ... few days after that gig. It wasn't Covid; I just ... it wasn't home anymore.
RADHA: That must've been ... really sad.
RYAN: Yeah, it was. Really sad. You find out who your friends are, that's for sure.
RADHA: And how did Pia take that?
RYAN: Oh, she stuck by me. I mean, she didn't have a choice, really. I was still transitioning and I was totally dependent on her financially. And she's been great. I mean, transitioning is like going through puberty again: for a while it was like we swapped roles and I was the one who was totally self-obsessed. And that was really hard on her. I couldn't talk about anything but trans stuff, to the point where anything she was going through emotionally, I just wasn't hearing it. Yeah, for a while I was off the charts.
RADHA: You got past it, though.
RYAN: With a lot of help, yeah. I actually thought ... we'd made it, you know? The serious emotional shit was behind us. I'd finished my course and I started working.
RADHA: Counselling.
RYAN: Yeah ... which brought in some money. Great thing about crisis counselling: no-one asks about your gender. You say your name is 'Ryan', that's all they need. And it takes you out of yourself, you know? I started listening to Pia again, to where she was at. I was ... feeling happy. Like I had a purpose. But then ... stupid as it sounds, I think what really fucked the chicken was top surgery. I was already pretty hairy by then, but once you get rid of the chesticles you really ... really start to look like a boy. And Pia is *so* not straight. And it was not just about the sex, either. Being a lesbian is—is ... it's a cultural thing. People were looking at us like a straight couple and that kinda meant that we didn't fit into a lot of our old social groups. I mean, no-one said that to our face, but ... yeah, more and more I was like this cage around her. So she's been going out on her own mostly, seeing other people ... I mean, I don't blame her. I can see it. She can't breathe ...

Beat.

Sorry. Ranting.
RADHA: No! No ... Really.

Beat.

What about—? What about your dad? Did he … ?

RYAN: Ah … Dad can't come at the whole trans thing. Just wants his butch daughter back … That's probably the worst part of it. We talk on the phone but … he doesn't … want to see me. Hilarious.

Beat.

RADHA: I think … you make a really nice boy.

RYAN: Thank you.

Pause.

Talking about my ex is probably not the greatest pick-up line, hey?

RADHA: I think you've got a lot to process.

RYAN: You don't wanna kiss me now, do you?

RADHA: I think you need some time.

RYAN: Mmm … That the only reason?

She hesitates.

Sorry. Don't … You don't have to answer.

RADHA: No! It's … I'm just weirded out right now. Not about you. Something happened earlier. That's all.

RYAN: Sure. Okay.

Beat.

With that guy? You came with?

She hesitates.

RADHA: I'm … just right now, not in a great headspace where men are concerned.

RYAN: Got it.

RADHA: I mean, it was no big deal.

RYAN: Okay.

RYAN *waits.*

RADHA: He put his hand up my dress. In the toilets.

RYAN: Oooh. Classy.

RADHA: He was a fuckhead.

RYAN: Yeah.

RADHA: He said he had some coke. I went in there, I did *one* line and then I feel his fucking hand on my crotch.

RYAN *grimaces.*

I tell him I'm spinning out and I wanna throw up … and he just keeps going! Until I have to actually fucking physically kick him off! I mean, what the fuck is wrong with him?

RYAN: Yeah. I get it.

RADHA: Why are men such fuckheads?

RYAN: Covered earlier, I think.

RADHA: I mean, you're not like that.

RYAN: Thank you.

RADHA: I think you're really, really nice.

RYAN: Yep. Thanks again.

RADHA: The way you listen, and ah …

He follows her gaze.

RYAN: You're … looking at my fly.

RADHA: Am I? No I'm not.

RYAN: Yeah, pretty sure you were.

RADHA: Definitely not.

An awkward beat.

I mean, not in a … It wasn't …

RYAN: It's a packer.

RADHA: It's a what?

RYAN: The bulge. It's a packer. A prosthetic.

RADHA: Oh. Okay.

RYAN: I can pee out of it and everything. I mean, it's my cock.

RADHA: Right. Of course … Wow, yeah, I did not … expect that.

RYAN: I don't have sex with it, though.

RADHA: Okay. Good to know.

Pause.

RYAN: You okay?

RADHA: Oh, yeah. Yes. I'm fine. Not worried about rape anymore.

RYAN: Oh. Cool. Great.

Beat.

And I guess we know why.

RADHA: Um … Stoned?

RYAN: No, it's ... same as my gig in the club. I haven't changed. You have changed me.
RADHA: Oh ... No! ... No, I haven't.
RYAN: We're still here, alone at night on the scary street ... Nothing different except how you see me.
RADHA: No, you—you were kind of weird before.
RYAN: And I'm not now?

She has to think.

RADHA: Okay. True.
RYAN: So ... ?
RADHA: I just—Okay, sure, you haven't changed. But now I know ... that you know ... how I feel. So I—I feel safe. That's it.
RYAN: Is that what it takes? To be transgender?
RADHA: What d'you mean?
RYAN: Trust. Empathy ... That's what it's about, right? Does a man actually have to be transgender before a woman can really trust him?
RADHA: That ... is a really good question. Maybe.
RYAN: Well, if he does then the human race is doomed.
RADHA: 'For I am human ... And I think nothing human is foreign to me.'
RYAN: Who said that?
RADHA: My dad. But he was quoting Terence.
RYAN: Oh, Terence. He works at the Oxford Tavern ... ?

She gives him a shove.

RADHA: No, it's ... Like you said, it's the middle of the night, we're alone ... Of course it's in the back of my mind. It's in the back of every woman's mind. But now I know you're okay, so ...
RYAN: Even though you know that you're safer on the street than a man is.
RADHA: Or you.
RYAN: Much safer than me.
RADHA: But that's in general. That's not here. Right now.
RYAN: No.

Beat.

RADHA: I feel like you wish I was afraid of you.
RYAN: No! No, fuck, no.
RADHA: If I was afraid of you, then you would feel like a real man.

RYAN: That's ... like I said, binary thinking. I am a real man. I don't have to prove it.
RADHA: No, but if I was afraid, then you'd know I see you that way. Completely as a man. Everyone would *see* you that way. You wouldn't be 'passing'. You would just be.

Beat.

Isn't that just another example of how insidious binary thinking is? How it colonises our imagination?
RYAN: I'm not trying to model myself on some ... binary archetype. I was born, I was not invented. I have a real father and to be honest, as a kid he's the one I modelled myself on. As you do. He's my dad.
RADHA: And now he only speaks to you on the phone.
RYAN: But that doesn't ... I can't just rip him out of my heart. Any more than you can rip your mum out of yours.

She looks at him.

RADHA: And how does he treat women?
RYAN: He looked after my mother till she died. He's a bogan. He has a mullet, he wears a leather jacket ... his mates are all bikies, or used to be. But he's the sort of bloke who steps into a fight to defend the weaker party. And he's exactly the type that you'd be scared of if you met him on a quiet street, late at night, after a party.

Pause.

Tell me something.
RADHA: What?
RYAN: Safe space.
RADHA: Totally safe. Ask away.
RYAN: What d'you think makes a real man?

She looks at him.

Because ever since I knew I was trans ... I have been asking myself, 'What is it, exactly, that I want to be?' I know I'm not my dad ... but it's a rabbit hole. The deeper I go, the more branches I take, the further I am from the answer. So, what d'you look for? As a woman.
RADHA: Oh ... shit. I don't know. The usual things.
RYAN: Like what?
RADHA: Kindness. Generosity. Loyalty ...

RYAN: And women don't have those?
RADHA: Of course! We all do.
RYAN: So you're saying that what you want … is a woman: a woman in a male body.
RADHA: I don't know … That'd be nice … No, I don't think so. But listen, it's a bullshit question. It's just your version of the usual identity crap that you ask yourself when you're going through a breakup. Your whole world is on a tilt.
RYAN: I had noticed.
RADHA: This—This will … In a month or so you'll realise that you've got it figured.
RYAN: Maybe. Maybe not. Indulge me.

Beat.

RADHA: Well … I just … I don't care, to be honest. I just want a good human being.
RYAN: Sure, but I'm not *asking* what makes a good human being. I'm asking, 'What makes a man?' Because … when you take away the binary norm … I can't figure it out.
RADHA: Why do you have to? I mean, it's a spectrum; that's what you were saying. Half the boys I know are playing with make-up and looking at fashion blogs, there are unisex toilets at school; who cares what part of it you fall into? Why do any of us have to be defined by gender?
RYAN: Because *I am a man*! I'm not playing at this! I'm not experimenting! I don't *feel* like I'm floating somewhere on a spectrum! I am not 'they' or 'xie' or 'hir'; I am '*he*', I am '*him*'. Because millions of years of evolution have made these … these roles! And they have meaning. And function. And I know there is a spectrum, I know, but … that part of it on the male end: I want that! I mean, I know what a woman is. You've defined that; you've been working on that since the nineteen sixties and you're still at it! Refining and defining and redefining and adjusting. But when you redefine women, you're also redefining men! Us! And sixty years later … what's left? How are we supposed to behave? I mean, cisgender boofheads getting smashed at the Kings Cross Hotel:

I can't identify with that, but what's the alternative? We're not breadwinners, or fighters or leaders or protectors anymore ... I get that, but what are we?

RADHA: Is that what you think women need? Protecting?

RYAN: Oh—says the chick who doesn't feel safe on the street at night.

RADHA *hesitates.*

I'm saying *we* need to *be* ... something! Something other than ... fucking ... misogynist goons. Sex pests and rapists and child abusers ... You think you're angry? Men are seriously confused and angry—but when men get angry they want to hurt someone because that's what they're built for, nature or nurture or whatever you want to call it. And mostly the first person they hurt is themselves.

RADHA: Well, maybe men should just fucking ... figure it out! You know that gender roles are not set in stone! You can't blame evolution. And I'm really, really sorry that you're feeling these things but women have been doing the hard slog for a bloody long time and ... we're only now just starting to work out who we want to be. Along with everyone else on the spectrum except for that little bit right on the end that represents so-called normal straight guys! So now you want *us* to figure out who *you* should be while we're at it? Well, I'm sorry but we don't really have the fucking time. Maybe the men that we love and respect and care about should just *do the fucking work.* And it's hard, I get it. And you feel lost. But it's necessary because we all share this planet and *we fucking need you*!

He looks at her.

You know? Maybe the reason Pia left is not because she was ... being pressured by the lesbian mafia. Maybe she just wanted you to grow up.

RYAN: Ah, great. Thanks.

RADHA: Sorry.

RYAN: Yeah, but ... not really.

Beat.

RADHA: No.

RYAN: So I guess this means you're not gunna call me.

Beat.

RADHA: I don't know.

That stings. He looks away.

RYAN: I probably do need some time.
RADHA: Me too.
RYAN: Oh, cute. 'Me too.' I see what you did there.
RADHA: Shut up.
BOYD: [*off*] Radha?

They are both startled. BOYD *enters. He's tall, athletic, good-looking. Dressed for a party, but not a themed one.*

RADHA: Boyd!
BOYD: You okay?
RYAN: Who's this?
RADHA: This is ... Boyd is the guy I came with.
RYAN: [*sizing him up*] Uh huh.
RADHA: [*to* BOYD] This is ... [*To* RYAN] Shit, I've forgotten your name.
RYAN: 'Ryan'.
RADHA: Sorry.
BOYD: But everything's okay?
RADHA: Yes! Yeah ... Thanks. We're talking about ... gender.
BOYD: Whoah. Deep.

BOYD *takes* RYAN *in.*

[*To* RADHA] So, what? You disappeared!
RADHA: Yeah ... I told you, I'm not feeling that well.
BOYD: Yeah, yeah, you did. You got a bit more colour now, though.
RADHA: I'm actually ...
BOYD: Got your second wind.
RADHA: No ... No, not really. Ryan's got an Uber coming.
BOYD: Ah, you'll be waiting all night. My car's just up the road; I'll drop you.
RADHA: Oh ... no, that's ...
BOYD: Yeah, yeah, Megan sent me a text.
RADHA: Magan?
BOYD: Yeah, yeah, Magan, she got your message. She can't make it, said I should drive you.

RADHA: Oh …
RYAN: Don't worry, mate, it's almost here.
>BOYD *turns. Beat.*
>She's on my way, so … no trouble.
>*He looks at* RADHA, *back at* RYAN.
BOYD: We met before?
RYAN: I don't think so.
BOYD: Look familiar.
>RYAN *shrugs.*
>[*To* RADHA] Fair enough. Your funeral.
>*They're hoping he will move on. He doesn't.*
>[*To both*] So what's up with gender? [*Holding up his hand*] I'm in favour.
>*No-one laughs.*
>Whoah. Tough crowd.
>*Headlights. A car approaches and a man shouts, 'Nice arse!' Followed by a beep on a musical horn.*
>[*Shouting back*] Hers or mine, shithead?
>*The car zooms on. He waves after them.*
>Fucking Bernie.
RADHA: We were talking about gendered violence.
BOYD: Oooh. Heavy.
RADHA: And how disrespect is on a spectrum that leads to assault.
>RYAN *and* BOYD *look at her. Beat.*
BOYD: Okay. Whatever.
RADHA: That's what I thought.
BOYD: It was just a fucking compliment, all right? Chill. Anyway, who says you got a nice arse? [*Nodding at* RYAN] It coulda been his.
RADHA: Funny.
BOYD: You got a bit sassy all of a sudden.
RADHA: Really.
BOYD: Is that 'cause I ran outta coke?

RADHA: Fuck off.
BOYD: [*to* RYAN] Fucking ... two hundred bucks lying on the shithouse floor thanks to this chick.
RYAN: Don't look at me. Sounds like you had it coming.
BOYD: [*looking from one to the other*] Ah, fuck, all right. I get it. [*To* RADHA] Look, I apologise, all right? I thought you were into it. You weren't. I get it. I'm sorry.
RADHA: You kept going when I told you to stop.
BOYD: I misinterpreted! ... Okay? But I'm clear now. I thought you were ... playing rough, that's all.

She looks at him.

Genuine apology! Honest to God. Fuck sake, why would Magan ask me to take you home if I wasn't straight-up?

She stares.

RADHA: All right, forget it.
BOYD: Okay.
RADHA: But tell your friend that was not a compliment.
BOYD: He didn't mean anything by it.
RADHA: I don't give a fuck! It felt like he did.
BOYD: Like what?
RADHA: Do I have to spell it out? Like I was an object that he could do what he wanted to. Like he wants to rape me.
BOYD: It was a joke! Fuck.
RADHA: It was disrespectful. And disrespect leads to dehumanisation. And dehumanisation leads to coercion and to violence.
BOYD: What the fuck? I disrespected right back at him! It doesn't mean I wanna rape 'im. Jesus.
RADHA: I'm not talking about you swapping trash-talk with your mates. This is a carload of anonymous fuckheads yelling 'Nice arse!' Or 'Slut!' Or 'Skank!' or whatever pearl happens to drop from their lips. If that's a joke I'm not getting it and I want you to tell him that it's not okay.

He looks at her, eyebrows raised, shrugs.

BOYD: All right, fuck, whatever. But maybe just see it from their point of view, okay?

RADHA: Their point of view? What would that be? The fuckhead perspective?
BOYD: Yeah, the fuckhead perspective. Look, I know these guys. They're not gunna rape anyone. They're just letting off steam.
RADHA: By making me feel like an object.
BOYD: He's not try'n'a make you feel anything. If *you* drove past *him* yelling 'Cocksucker', he'd give you the middle finger, but he wouldn't be thinking, 'Oh, fuck, no, I've been objectified'. Where he comes from, that's passing the time of day. Right? You and him see things differently. Don't take it personal.
RADHA: It's personal when it's sexualised.
BOYD: Why? What difference does it make? Like, if some chick wolf-whistled me in the street, I'd just think it was cute, right?
RADHA: That is *completely*—
BOYD: Whatever. I'm just saying he's treating you the way he's happy for you to treat him. And maybe that's dumb but there's nothing violent in it. Get off your rocking horse.
RADHA: Until there is … Until I say 'No' and it keeps happening. And they think it's funny. Or they think they can bully me into fucking them. Or until I happen to be that last woman … on a long line of abused women … who gets a punch in the face instead of a foul word.
BOYD: Oh, fuck, Jesus. You are on a real downer.
RYAN: Why don't you listen to what she's saying? She's telling you something.
BOYD: Jesus Christ, no-one is getting raped around here! Okay? [*To* RADHA] I'm sorry I got it wrong before but it was just a misunderstanding! Don't burn me at the stake for it. Jesus, I'm just a boy. I don't know anything.

RADHA *looks at him, but she knows she's pushing shit uphill.*

RADHA: Fine.
BOYD: [*indicating* RYAN] And thanks for telling this dickhead, by the way.
RADHA: Well, maybe don't grab random women and there won't be anything to report.
BOYD: Okay. All right, I get it. [*To* RYAN] Way to end a party, eh?

BOYD *looks at him.*

I know I seen you round.

RYAN: At the party maybe.

BOYD: Yeah, yeah, yeah … You're Nico's mate.

RYAN: Nah, don't think so.

BOYD: No?

RYAN: No, I came with my girlfriend. Don't know anybody.

BOYD: Huh … Who's your girlfriend?

RYAN: Miranda.

RADHA *glances at him. The name means nothing to* BOYD.

BOYD: Mmm. Weird. [*To* RADHA] Anyway, am I driving you home or what? Because Magan did ask me and that Uber could be on its way to fucking outer space.

RADHA *looks at* RYAN. *He checks his phone.*

RYAN: Still in Glebe. Not moving. I can re-book.

BOYD: Fuck no. Come on. That's my car just there.

RADHA: Are you okay to drive?

BOYD: Yeah, yeah … Two beers, that's it.

RYAN: And a line of coke.

BOYD: Yeah, cancels out the beers.

RADHA *looks from one to the other.* RYAN *doesn't like the feel of this.*

RYAN: I'll re-book it.

RADHA: Let me call her again.

BOYD: Sure, go for your life.

RADHA *takes out her phone and walks off.* BOYD *waits until she's out of earshot.*

Pretty sure I know you.

RYAN: Nah, I think I'd remember.

BOYD: Yeah, yeah, yeah.

Beat.

Listen, mate, I'm not crowding you or something?

RYAN: How d'you mean?

BOYD: [*nodding after* RADHA] You know. Crowding.

RYAN *looks at him.*

RYAN: We're just talking.

BOYD: Yeah? Cool … She's pretty fucking dark on me all of a sudden. I picked her up at this other party.

RYAN: Yeah, she said.

BOYD: Yeah? … Fuck, the magic was happening, mate. Then I said I knew I could get some blow at this one and I swear, she was hot to trot.

RYAN: Okay.

BOYD: [*holding his fingertips close together*] This close to a fucking blowjob. I swear. Anyway, she's a cranky bitch but I seriously want to bang her, she is hot.

RYAN: What?

BOYD: You didn't see her before, I'm telling you. Just gotta talk my way into her place and she'll be up for it. Seriously.

RYAN *stares at him.*

RYAN: What about her flatmates?

BOYD: Well, Megan's with a mate of mine right now; she's not coming back, that's a cert. And she told me the other ones are visiting family in Geelong or somewhere.

RYAN: Mate … you've missed your moment. She doesn't want to have anything to do with you. Plus she is fried … She's not in a good state to consent.

BOYD: I know, but look at the arse on her! Fuck …

RYAN: Boyd … get in your car now and drive away.

BOYD *stares at him, grins.*

BOYD: Oooh, yeah, that's what I thought.

RYAN *looks at him. What?*

You'd like that. If I left her with you. We're not so different.

BOYD *sucks his teeth for a second.*

I do know you.

RYAN *stares.*

RYAN: Know how to get your way, don't you?

BOYD: I do all right.

RYAN: Top dog. I mean, a dominant male. Other men look at you and … they kind of feel like they have to go along. Run with the pack.

    BOYD *looks at him.*

If I put my hand on your arse right now, how'd you go with that?
BOYD: What the fuck?
RYAN: It's a great arse. I'm just saying. Let me give it a good squeeze.
BOYD: Let me give you a good smack in the head.
RYAN: Yeah? Just 'cause I cop a feel? That's a bit extreme. You'd never make a woman, Boyd. Can dish it out, can't take it.

    The stare at one another.

You know what happens when you get a smack in the head? All you want to do is get up. Recover. Get moving. But if you get raped … you just wanna crawl into a corner and never move again. A woman doesn't 'get over' being raped, Boyd. It's in her. Forever.
BOYD: When did I say I was gunna rape her?
RYAN: Just part of the unwritten code, isn't it? It's not rape if we don't say it. But I'm not backing you on this one, Boyd. Not gunna pretend that what you're doing is fine when I know it's not. Sorry I don't wanna be in your gang. Not one of the boys.

    BOYD *sucks his teeth for a second.*

BOYD: Pussy.
RYAN: Not afraid of that, either. You know where good-looking cisgender men like you and gay men have common cause?
BOYD: Can't guess.
RYAN: In prison. They're both afraid of getting fucked. I think you want to stay out of prison, Boyd.
BOYD: Me? … I'm not the one facing charges.

    Beat.

Remember Janine? She remembers you.
RYAN: I have never seen you before.
BOYD: Yeah, yeah, yeah, you fucking have. You were pissed, but, eh?

    RYAN *stares at him. He does remember.*

I guess you don't tell everybody you're a girl.
RYAN: I'm not.

BOYD: Matter of opinion.
RYAN: Nope. Just how it is.
BOYD: Not how Janine tells it.
RYAN: Not my problem.
BOYD: Not a man. Not a woman. What are you?
RYAN: I'm a better man than you.

> BOYD *lashes out and punches* RYAN *in the face.* RYAN *staggers back, holding his nose.*

BOYD: What about now? Still better than me?

> BOYD *punches him again.*

Still feeling it? Eh? Faggot?
RADHA: [*off*] Boyd! ... Stop! Boyd!

> RADHA *enters, holding her phone.*

Stop now! Leave him alone!
BOYD: Oh, he deserves it. He raped a friend of mine.

A stunned beat.

RYAN: [*cupping his bruised face*] That is *bullshit*!
BOYD: Not what she says.
RADHA: He—? He raped—?
RYAN: It did not happen!
BOYD: She went to the cops, mate.
RYAN: I don't give a fuck!
BOYD: You say she's lying?
RADHA: Boyd ... that is ridiculous!
BOYD: They're investigating. As we speak.

> RADHA *looks at* RYAN.

RYAN: They have to. It doesn't mean it happened.
BOYD: He got her smashed, took her to the bedroom in my mate's house—
RYAN: I didn't ... She—She was fine to consent.
BOYD: Digitally penetrated her ...
RYAN: Shut the fuck up!
BOYD: Forgot to mention one little thing.
RYAN: I thought she knew! I thought ... We were talking all *night* ...
BOYD: But she didn't.

RYAN: So what? Do you go around telling chicks, 'By the way, just so you know, I have a penis?'
BOYD: I don't have to, mate. I'm still how God made me.
RYAN: We went to the bedroom, she changed her mind ... I left. How is that rape?
BOYD: It's a rape because *she* felt violated. And I choose to believe her. Not the guy who raped her.
RYAN: *I didn't fucking rape her!*
BOYD: Find out in court, I guess.
RYAN: It'll never get to court!
BOYD: Time will tell, hey. [*To* RADHA] But I'm driving you home. I don't want this deviant anywhere near you.

> RADHA *looks from one to the other.* RYAN *shakes his head.*

RYAN: [*to* RADHA] No, no ... Don't go with him. Please.

> RADHA *eases her phone into a pocket.*

Radha. Walk home if you want. Go to your mum's place ...
BOYD: Oh, nice. And what then? You follow her?
RYAN: Oh, you cunt.

> BOYD *shoves him.*

RADHA: Boyd!

> *Beat.*

[*To* RYAN] She reported you? To the police?

> RYAN *stares.*

BOYD: Women don't lie about getting raped.
RYAN: She's not lying!

> *Beat.*

[*To* RADHA, *hopelessly*] She got it wrong.

> BOYD *grins.*

BOYD: Gotta believe the victim, though, yeah? [*To* RADHA] He's a piece of shit. Let's go.

> BOYD *leads the way.* RADHA *doesn't move.*

What?

> RADHA *looks at him.*

RADHA: Thanks, but … you go. I'm fine.

    BOYD *hesitates.*

BOYD: Say again?
RADHA: I don't think I want you to drive me home. But thanks.
BOYD: This guy … tried to fuck my mate's girlfriend … without telling her he was trans!
RADHA: And why the fuck should he? He's a human being. So is she. If she freaks out over that, it's her problem. It's not rape.
BOYD: You're seriously siding with this faggot?
RADHA: You make it so easy.
BOYD: He's a fucking girl! You know that.
RADHA: And you are a narcissistic, homophobic cunt with wandering hands. So don't be hating.
BOYD: You're a fucking bitch.
RADHA: Gold-plated. So, take it to the bank, fuckhead.

    BOYD *looks from one to the other.*

You going to punch him again? Or you want to slap me first?
BOYD: You two cunts deserve each other.

    BOYD *exits towards his car. They watch until the door slams, and the car drives off.* RYAN *sits in the gutter, tries to breathe.*

RADHA: What happened to our safe space?

    She joins RYAN, *examines his face.*

RYAN: You are … Yeah. Wow.
RADHA: I'm taking you to hospital.
RYAN: No … that's … It's—I've had worse.
RADHA: Really?
RYAN: Oh … yeah. It'll tighten up tomorrow but it's not too bad. If he hadn't king-hit me I think I could've taken him.
RADHA: Surprised you didn't. You move like a trained boxer.
RYAN: Do I?
RADHA: No.

    He smirks. Beat.

RYAN: I'll tell you what's never happened before, though.
RADHA: What's that?
RYAN: Someone stopped it.

She looks at him, touches his face. Headlights approach and RADHA *suddenly jumps up, waving.*

RADHA: Oh, my God! It's your Uber!

The car pulls over and she helps RYAN *to his feet.*

RYAN: I'm taking you to your mum's place.

RADHA: Don't be such a fucking boy. We're going to hospital, then we're calling the police.

RYAN: Ah, no … forget it.

RADHA: Forget it?

RYAN: No point.

RADHA: So he gets to go home, sleep it off and carry on tomorrow like it never happened.

He looks at her.

And next time? When he finds someone else to punch in the face?

RYAN: They won't charge him. He'll deny it ever happened.

RADHA: I'm a witness.

RYAN: And I'm a trans guy with a rape allegation.

RADHA: [*holding up her phone*] Also I might have … recorded it. Like people do.

He looks at her, shakes his head, smiling.

RYAN: Still won't make it to court.

RADHA: Don't give a shit. At least he gets a few sleepless nights.

RYAN: You're delusional.

RADHA: The point is, you have a right. We have a right. To be ourselves. To be here. In this place. At this time. And be safe. So just … fucking, shut the fuck up.

They move towards their Uber.

RYAN: Any chance you'll call me after this?

RADHA: Oh, because you show me such a good time.

RYAN: I said I'm an enigma.

RADHA: You're a cosmic arsehole. Just get in the car.

They exit towards the headlights.

THE END

Straight White Male

April 23 - May 5, 2024 at La Mama HQ

Norm and Ahmed written by Alex Buzo

Norm Danny McGinlay
Ahmed Isaac Rajakariar

Radha and Ryan written by Nick Parsons

Radha Gursimar Kaur
Ryan Sam Eade
Boyd Danny McGinlay

Director Nick Parsons
Designer Joanna Arrowsmith
Lighting Designer Max Bowyer
Sound Designer Mikaela Innes
Music Thomas Smith

LA MAMA THEATRE: FACILITATING FEARLESSLY INDEPENDENT THEATRE-MAKING.

Founded in 1967, La Mama is Australia's most vital, responsive, inclusive and diverse home of independent theatre-making. We believe in the power and possibilities of theatre and art for all people.

La Mama engages audiences as a community and offers affordable and hospitable cultural experiences that appeal to a broad range of people.

Each year at La Mama, two thousand artists develop their practice, are given their first opportunity and have their finest performance moment. Hundreds of new Australian works have been generated over the decades.

Annually we present 40+ Australian premieres, participate in festivals (Midsumma, Comedy, Fringe, Yirramboi) and present our own festivals & programs: First Nations, Festival of Mother Tongue (LOTE), Puppet Festival, quarterly children and multi-arts (poetry, cabaret, music, scratch), Explorations (works in development), Emerge (Youth), Online and Pathways.

We exist to nurture and amplify all Australian voices.

Photograhs by Glenn Hester Photography

WRITER AND DIRECTOR'S NOTE

The Australia of my childhood feels like a quieter, safer place than the one I live in today. As a people I remember Australians as more unified and happier. And yet, by any statistical measure, it was in fact more violent, less equal, more unjust and less diverse than the society we live in today.

How have we become simultaneously more isolated and more fearful, yet better connected and safer? Our incredible digital revolution has given us instant access to these facts and statistics, and to each other through multiple portals. Marginalised people who once suffered alone can now find each other and identify common cause – yet the same technology encourages us to demonise others and polarise our society.

Often when I write drama I find myself playing devil's advocate. It's the writer's curse: no character is a villain to themselves. A powerful story requires a powerful antagonist, someone convinced they are the hero of their own life. And often the most morally dubious characters are the most fascinating, for that very reason.

I would describe myself as a feminist ally, but I'm also a straight, cisgender white male of a certain age. I knew I wanted to write something about how feminism and diversity politics is forcing a revolution in male identity, and how some men are being left in its wake ... but an idea is not a premise. I had no idea who would people my story or what the action might be. So the project remained dormant for a year or so until, in a conversation with my very brilliant agent in 2021, I hit upon the idea of using the same premise as Alex Buzo's New Wave classic, *Norm and Ahmed*: a straight, white man accosting an Asian student late at night, near a bus stop. The time and location alone set up an expectation of violence. But in my play the student would be a young, vulnerable woman. My two characters could have a wide-ranging conversation about sex, gender and discrimination, and their own surprising histories, and all the time dramatic momentum is maintained by the unspoken questions – is this man who he says he is, what does he really want, and what will he do?

Producing the play with *Norm and Ahmed* seemed a natural choice.

The plays echo each other, unified by the theme of masculine identity on the cusp of change. They are both set at a bus stop, late at night, both observe the unities of time, place and action, and both require a small cast.

I'm grateful to Emma Buzo for allowing *Norm and Ahmed* on the program. It caused a storm of controversy when it was first performed in 1968, triggering a change in our outdated censorship laws. Today I feel safe in calling it a modern classic. I have no idea how *Radha and Ryan* will be received. Just as with *Norm and Ahmed* there is content that some will find offensive. To them I apologise. My only excuse is that in order to write about polarising issues, my characters must at times say some polarising things.

Of course, every play is a journey, and *Radha and Ryan* has come a long way from its premise. It started as a play about two characters struggling to topple each other from the highest moral ground. But I hope it has resolved into a plea for unity in our diversity, for conversation over condemnation. As Terence put it, 'For I am a human being, and I think nothing human is foreign to me'.

There are many wonderful people who have helped me bring this play to the stage. Some are in the acknowledgements, and their contribution cannot be overstated, but I must also thank my family, who have supported me in this production, particularly my wife Jo, who is my sounding board and also the set and costume designer, my daughter Ade who is assisting, my nephew composer Thomas Smith and my brother in law Peter Smith, who has volunteered for the bump-in and bump-out. And of course I am forever grateful to our brilliant cast and crew, and the wonderful people at La Mama, who are unrelated to me, but showed their faith in this play and gave their time for the love of the work, and of theatre – which is what drives us all.

Nick Parsons, 6 April, 2024

NICK PARSONS
PLAYWRIGHT / DIRECTOR

Nick is a writer and director in film, television theatre and radio. He has a BA (hons) in Philosophy from Sydney University and is a graduate of both the Australian Film, Television and Radio School and the National Institute of Dramatic Art, completing the directing and writing courses concurrently in both institutions. His stage plays include *The Pest House*, *Dead Heart*, *Hollow Ground* and the musical *A Nasty Piece of Work*. He wrote and directed the feature film *Dead Heart* (1996), based on his play, as well as *The Saviour* (2006), a half-hour episode of the TV series two *Twisted*, and *Tipping Point* (2007) a 16-part mini-doc series for The Weather Channel. He has directed numerous plays and also written episodes of the TV series *My Place* (2010, 2011), *The Straits* (2012), and *Wolf Creek 2* (2017). In development in 2024 are the feature film *Narcisse* and a number of TV projects. His awards and nominations include: **2012** Deadly Award (with others), Best TV Series for *The Straits*; AWGIE (with others), best TV Drama Series for *The Straits* **2011** Logie (with others), Best Children's TV series for *My Place* season two; AWGIE, Best Episode of Children's Drama for *My Place* '1868 – Minna' **2010** Logie (with others), Best Children's TV series for *My Place* season one; The Queensland Premier's Literary Award nomination, TV Drama for *My Place*: '1978 – Mike' **2007** ASTRA nomination, Most Outstanding Short-Form Program for documentary series *Tipping Point* **2001** AWGIE nomination, Best Stage Play for *Hollow Ground* **1996** Film Critics Circle Award, Best Adapted Screenplay for the film *Dead Heart*; AFI nomination, Best Adapted Screenplay for the film *Dead Heart* **1993** The Australian

Human Rights Award for the stage play *Dead Heart*; The NSW Premier's Literary Award for the stage play *Dead Heart*; 1993 AWGIE, Best Stage Play for *Dead Heart* **1988** The Ian Reed Memorial Grand Prize for radio drama for *The White Room* **1986** AFI nomination, Best Short Film for *The Portrait of Wendy's Father*.

ALEX BUZO
PLAYWRIGHT

ALEX BUZO was born in Sydney. He was educated at the Armidale School, the International School in Geneva and the University of New South Wales from which he graduated with a BA in 1965. In 2005 he was awarded an Honorary Doctorate of Letters from the University of New South Wales for his contribution to Australian literature. In 1968, Buzo's first play *Norm and Ahmed* was among the first to find a truly Australian voice and gained national attention primarily through a prosecution for obscenity. The exploration of alienation in this play remained a common theme in his work, often delivered with clever and stylish use of the Australian idiom and a tireless commitment to reflecting the true nature of Australian society. In 1972, Buzo was awarded the Australian Literature Society's Gold Medal for his play *Macquarie*. His plays include *Rooted*, *The Front Room Boys*, *Coralie Lansdowne Says No*, *Martello Towers*, *Makassar Reef*, *Big River*, *The Marginal Farm*, *Shellcove Road* and *Pacific Union*. His work has been produced around the world including the USA, the UK and South East Asia. He was also writer-in-residence at many theatre companies, schools and universities. Following Buzo's death in 2006, his daughter Emma founded the Alex Buzo Company in 2007.

GURSIMAR KAUR
RADHA

Gursimar Kaur is an Indian actress based in Naarm / Melbourne. She found a passion for performing at the age of four when she started learning various Indian dance styles. Her desire for performing extended throughout high school, encouraging her to attend the Arts Academy, Federation University, graduating with a Bachelor of Performing Arts (2023). During her studies she has been a part of various projects including *Into the Woods* (Jack's Mother), directed by Alister Smith, *Metamorphosis* (various characters), directed by Dr Ross Hall. Since graduating, Gursimar was a part of the web-series *Jaffy's* (Zarina) produced by Screen Australia, directed by Haley Adams.

SAM EADE
RYAN

Sam Eade is a transgender male actor based in Naarm / Melbourne and a Victorian College of the Arts Graduate (2023). Sam grew up doing gymnastics and went on to play a long list of other sports such as rowing, swimming and diving. After graduating high school Sam continued to explore his passion for sports by studying a year at Deakin, but eventually went on to study at the Victorian College of the Arts (VCA). His VCA credits include Romeo and various roles in *Palace of Illusions* (dir. Sonya Suares), Rob in *New Labour* (dir. Alice Qin), Theo in *Roulette* (dir. Tony Nikolakopoulas), Hugh in *All Boys* (dir. Max Tassell) and Miles in *She Kills Monsters* (dir. Joe Paradise Lui). Since graduating, earlier this year Sam performed at the Motley Bauhaus in *Perpetual Stew* (dir. Milly Walker and Charles Lawrence).

DANNY MCGINLAY
NORM / BOYD

A Stand-Up Comedian by trade. Danny has performed on four continents, gigged for Prime Ministers, Royalty and even Arnold Schwarzenegger. He's pivoted to more acting since the pandemic and has been seen on *Fisk*, *Utopia* and that Toyota Ad that was on all the time.

ISAAC RAJAKARIAR
AHMED

Isaac Rajakariar is a Tamil-Australian actor based in Naarm / Melbourne. He discovered his passion for acting while performing in high school theatre productions and after a brief stint studying economics at university, he decided he'd much rather navigate the entertainment industry than the corporate world. Since graduating from The Australian Film and Television Academy (TAFTA) in 2021, Isaac has performed in anti-racism campaigns for the Vietnamese Community of Australia and more recently in the Breeding Ground Productions feature film *Residence*. Isaac has a love for comedy, cartoons, and calliteration and hopes he never finds a reason to finish his economics degree.

JOANNA ARROWSMITH
DESIGNER

Joanna Arrowsmith won the combined Universities Art Exhibition whilst a student at La Trobe University in the '70s. She has taught Literature and History at many institutions and lectured in Comparative Politics and Political Philosophy at the University of Technology Sydney. She has a Diploma of Production Design and a BA (Film & and Television) from the Australian Film, Television and Radio School where she was a Directing student. Her two short films, *The Silence of Peig O'Bede* and *Conversations with a Dead Man*, which she wrote, designed and directed, both won Best Film Awards in consecutive years at the Toowoomba Film Festival. She is an artist and designer with a focus on heritage architecture.

MAX BOWYER
LIGHTING DESIGNER

Max Bowyer (He/Him), is a Set / Lighting designer and maker for live performance based in Naarm (Melbourne). With a Bachelor of Fine Arts (Production) under his belt, Max draws inspiration from the intricacies of space, human motivations, and innovative technology. His passion for live performance stems from the vital nature of storytelling, and his unwavering drive for world-building. Max's journey into live performance design began with his profound appreciation for theatre and music theatre, where the fusion of storytelling, architecture, design, and creative problem-solving drives his systematic, collaborative approach.

MIKAELA INNES
SOUND DESIGNER

Mikaela grew up in Boorloo (Perth, Western Australia) and in 2019 relocated to Naarm (Melbourne, Victoria), and is a recent graduate of the Australian Institute of Music (Bachelor of Music, Music Theatre). During their time at AIM, Mikaela played Logainne in *The 25th Annual Putnam County Spelling Bee* (dir. Johanna Allen), Macduff in *Macbeth* (dir. Rachel Baring) and found great purpose in devising their solo show, *The 5 Stages of Christmas*. Passionate about new theatre—especially for young audiences—they have been privileged to work with Polyglot Theatre (through Wyndham City Arts and Culture), host the 2022 Vision Australia Carols by Candlelight Kids' Preshow, play the role of Klaus—a talking rabbit—in *Bayou Bart* at Theatre Works (dir. Kalina Lauer) and of Slacks—an anthropomorphised pair of pants—in Wesley Middleton's *Unsorted* (Theatre Works, Midsumma Festival, dir. Tara Daniel), and puppeteer the albatross Dave in *Owl and the Albatross* (Theatre Works, dir. Sarah Branton / Paris Balla). When not creating, Mikaela can be found in the management side of productions and events. Most recently she has Stage Managed for A Blanck Canvas and was engaged as Co-Stage Manager for Teeth and Tonic at La Mama Courthouse. They also Production Managed *The White Rose: in Concert* at Gasworks Arts Park (Isabella Dymovoloski / Oliver Thomson) and was invited back to AIM to Stage Manage *Pippin* (dir. Johanna Allen).

THOMAS SMITH
MUSIC

Thomas Smith is an Eora / Sydney-based artist, musician, educator and researcher. His practice combines performance, video, electronic music, speculative fiction, websites, curatorial projects and critical writing. Thomas' work is concerned with the social effects of computational systems, the politics of creative economies, emerging digital subjectivities and electronic music as a mode critical inquiry. Thomas is also one half of production duo Utility, and runs independent record label Sumactrac with Jarred Beeler (DJ Plead) and Jon Watts.

www.currency.com.au

Visit Currency Press' website now to:
- Buy your books online
- Browse through our full list of titles, from plays to screenplays, books on theatre, film and music, and more
- Choose a play for your school or amateur performance group by cast size and gender
- Obtain information about performance rights
- Find out about theatre productions and other performing arts news across Australia
- For students, read our study guides
- For teachers, access syllabus and other relevant information
- Sign up for our email newsletter

The performing arts publisher

www.ingramcontent.com/pod-product-compliance
Lightning Source LLC
Chambersburg PA
CBHW042130160426
43198CB00022B/2970